UNLEASHED!

UNLEASHED!

Expecting Greatness and Other Secrets of Coaching for Exceptional Performance

Gregg Thompson
with Susanne Biro

SelectBooks, Inc.

Unleashed!: Expecting Greatness and Other Secrets of Coaching for Exceptional Performance
© 2006 by Gregg Thompson

This edition published by SelectBooks, Inc., New York, New York.

First Edition

ISBN-13: 978-1-59079-113-4

ISBN-10: 1-59079-113-4

Library of Congress Cataloging-in-Publication Data

Thompson, Gregg, 1950–

Unleashed! : Expecting greatness and other secrets of coaching for exceptional perform-ance / Gregg Thompson with Susanne Biro. -- 1st ed.

   p. cm.

Includes bibliographical references and index.

ISBN-13: 978-1-59079-113-4 (hardbound cover : alk. paper)
ISBN-10: 1-59079-113-4

1. Employees--Coaching of. 2. Employee motivation. I. Biro, Susanne, 1973– II. Title.

HF5549.5.C53T46 2007

658.3'124--dc22

2006036615

Manufactured in the United States of America

10 9 8 7 6 5 4 3 2 1

This book is dedicated to
the memory of Boyd Clarke,
our partner, friend and coach,
who challenged us to
"help others become the
very best version of themselves."

Contents

Complimentary Online Coaching Assessment

Each reader of **Unleashed!** is entitled to receive a personalized Leader as Coach Inventory (LCI) report. The LCI is an online assessment designed to provide you with confidential feedback on your coaching practices and coaching potential from a group of individuals whom you select. These individuals will anonymously rate you on how frequently you engage in 30 coach-like behaviors and will also comment on how you have "*Earned the Right to Coach*," created "*Perfect Partnerships*," and engaged in "*Dangerous Conversations*." The LCI is designed to provide you with positive, constructive information that you will probably never receive elsewhere. The ratings and commentary contained in the LCI can greatly influence your development as a coach and a leader. We strongly encourage you to take advantage of this opportunity.

To initiate the LCI process, simply go to
www.bluepointleadership.com/unleashed/lci
and enter the following code#:

IWALS

Once your report is complete, it will be sent to you via email.

Acknowledgments

So many people have contributed to this book and, indeed, to our lives. These are people who cared enough to challenge us and to hold us accountable to make our lives meaningful. To all of you, even those unnamed, we thank you and will be forever grateful.

Shepherding a book like this from inception to publication is no easy task and it would not have happened without the inspiration, editing, proofreading, and cajoling of Kenzi Sugihara, Dana Isaacson, Emily Bolton, Mary Jo Dionne, Bonnie Gale, Helen Miller and Khim Goh. Special thanks go to Keith McLeod, Jim Suttie and Scott Burbank for generously sharing their coaching stories.

From Susanne:

I am so very grateful for my incredible parents, Elfie and Geza Biro, who always said "you will go places," and made me believe them, and to my two beautiful sisters, Judy and Sharon, who continually show me what true kindness is. I would also like to thank my business mentor and friend, John Rose, for always making time for me and for continuing to challenge me to become what I do not yet believe I can be. To my partner on this project, Gregg: I am in awe of your grace and wisdom. I have learned what exceptional leadership is from your example, and you have forever changed who I believe I am. I would like to thank Chris, Rachel, Robyn, Stacey, Stacy and Jim; your support, coaching and love over the last two years has been the rock that has allowed me to learn, write and work in ways I had not thought possible. And to the authors whose work has inspired me: Tim Sanders, Eckhart Tolle, Wayne Dyer and Ann Coombs, thank you for helping me believe that love is power.

From Gregg:

My life has been indelibly etched by the compassion, faith and sacrifice expressed every day by my father, Ruben, and my wonderful step-mother, Marie; my sisters Sharon and Linda and my brother Evert; my wife, Judy, and our three spectacular sons, Jason, Joel and Jonathan. I would also like to thank two of my very best friends, Don and Bea Nyberg. I am honored to work with some of the finest coaches, facilitators and business professionals on the planet. I particularly want to thank my partners at Bluepoint Leadership Development, Ron Crossland, David Parks, Bryn Meredith and Ng Weng Jun, who demand the very best of me, our organization, our clients and themselves. Nancy, Keira and Jamie, thank you for holding it all together. There are many outstanding leadership coaches in the world but, like that rare fine wine, occasionally one comes along who lifts the bar for the rest of us. My collaborator, Susanne, is just such a coach.

We are both particularly grateful to our clients. Thank you for trusting us with your challenges and your dreams. We are continually in awe of your courage and passion as you strive to become the very best versions of yourselves.

Foreword

One of the most frequently quoted passages from Anne Morrow Lindbergh's graceful, slim book *Gift from the Sea* is, "Good communication is as stimulating as black coffee and just as hard to sleep after." Thompson and Biro provide us with terrific coaching constructs; wonderful, practical tools (which adults appear to demand from business books); and insights into the best practices of exceptional coaches. They do not achieve this through academic presentation, pontification, reducing great ideas to fable-sized sound bites, or through that popular form of inspirational business evangelism used by some popular pundits. It is done with a far more accessible communication approach. Reading this book is like having a conversation with a friend by the sea. Be prepared for a difficult few nights of sleep.

It is a dangerous conversation—as the authors point out that, "Telling the truth is a perilous endeavor." And Thompson tells the truth—every hard-won ounce of truth he has learned over the difficult, delightful, and dangerous years of being a highly respected (and well-paid) executive coach. For many who read this book, the dangerous truth he will convey to you will concern not how to coach, but how to prepare yourself to be a coach. You will be invited to traverse the important arc from the truth about who you are as a Leader Coach to the truth about how you can best coach your Talent to unleash his or her own might. To unleash talent, you must first unleash yourself.

Coaching is not casual. It is not about one expert helping another tool up to their level of expertise. Borrowing well-selected quotes from psychologists, philosophers, poets, leadership experts and the occasional sports coach, various threads of wisdom are woven into something altogether new. This conversation reframes the familiar.

There are many wonderful, immediately practical application ideas in the "Try This" sidebars you will find peppered throughout. My encouragement: try one. By reading this book you will be provided a rare opportunity as a manager, leader, counselor, teacher, sponsor, parent, or coach to test these constructs through imminently practical applications that you can act upon in short order. In our microwave, instant gratification world it doesn't get much better than this.

I set a goal after graduating college to read 2,000 books during my adult life with the notion that one book might not improve my mind, but many might. This book is an exception to that notion. *Unleashed!* alone uplifted my mind about coaching. After reading it, the best "Try This" I can suggest is:

Buy two copies of this book. Read one and have your coach read the other. Then get together and have a conversation about coaching.

Ron Crossland
In flight over North America
September, 2006

Introduction

I was twenty years old and in college when I realized that I was really quite ordinary. By then, the damage had already been done. I had spent the first two decades of my life under the delusion that I was special. Who was to blame? My mother, of course. It was all her fault. At an early age, she took me aside and told me secrets, secrets which I promised to reveal to no one. *"You are very, very smart; you'll probably be the smartest boy in the school. You must be careful not to lord this over others. You will also have many friends, probably too many. You must do your best to spend time with each of them and help them in any way you can. I've also noticed that you are very fast, probably the fastest in the neighborhood. You must help others run just as fast."* By the time I was ten years old, my mother's perspective on my abilities had taken complete control of my life. I marched into school thinking I was smart, waded into relationships believing I was likable, and tried out for sports teams convinced I was athletic.

As I look back now at these three aspects of my life—academics, relationships, and athletics—I can see how blessed I was with rich experiences. They were not always perfect. I did not always make the honor roll. Sometimes I was rejected by those I considered friends. I was cut from sports teams I desperately wanted to make. But I dove into these endeavors with the confidence that I could succeed, if not this time, then next time for sure. And I succeeded more times than my limited abilities should have allowed. My mother gave me many gifts during her life but none as precious as the gift of Great Expectations.

So what does this have to do with a book on coaching? Management futurists are fond of predicting a "War for Talent." They foresee a time in the near future when organizations will be battling for their very survival in the arena of top performers. I agree that organizations will increasingly face debilitating shortages of talent; however, I also believe that this war can be fought and won primarily *within* organizations. Look around your organization right now—in its cubicles and inside its hallways, in its meeting rooms and labs, on its factory floor. Any place where people work you will find enormous, untapped potential waiting to be developed and deployed. No need for headhunters or expensive recruitment campaigns. Talent is everywhere; it just needs to be unleashed! This is the job of the Leader as Coach. It's *your* job. And my mother had the recipe: seek out the very best in people and challenge them to live up to their own Great Expectations!

Coaching has received a great deal of attention over the last several years. As today's fastest growing human resource development process, coaching is quickly becoming an essential competency for leaders at every organizational level. Where once it was seen as an ancillary supervisory skill, today's talent-starved organizations are demanding that all leaders be able to coach for high performance. Why? Quite simply because coaching produces such impressive results. When carried out well, it produces remarkable improvement in the performance of individuals. No other development process—from formal education to online learning—comes close.

It is actually quite easy to see why coaching is such a potent approach to performance improvement. When people have the opportunity to reflect on their unique aspirations and talents, receive one-on-one attention from an attentive and genuinely interested manager, and are encouraged to create their own development plans, they are highly motivated to change.

As we navigate through our careers, most of our learning and development comes from those demanding endeavors that require us to stretch our thinking and abilities the furthest. High performance coaching accelerates this process by helping the person create the challenging developmental experiences necessary to reach this level of achievement.

In the last few years, coaching has moved away from being the exclusive domain of professional coaches. Now, leaders at all levels are being asked to become more coach-like with their team members and colleagues. And yet, despite its growing popularity, certain misconceptions about coaching are pervasive. Contrary to the popular view, coaching is not a nice, neat cognitive process involving the exchange of feedback, insights, and action plans. It might better be described as a muddled, awkward expedition full of chaos, experimentation, self-learning, disappointment, and elation. And coaching is certainly not easy. It requires a considerable investment of time and energy to help another learn and develop. Unfortunately, many of us who lead organizations have little experience with, or training in, the processes which distinguish true coaching from an ordinary conversation. As a result, we find ourselves ill-equipped to do what is now being asked of us. It's not that we lack the requisite interpersonal and leadership abilities. It's simply that high performance coaching demands more than the basic communication and interpersonal practices such as relating well to others and providing constructive feedback. Coaching is not about doing more of the same traditional management practices. It's about building intense, development-focused relationships and engaging in risky, performance-changing conversations.

It's likely that, without giving it a name, you have been the recipient of great coaching at some point in your career. Consider for a moment your own career successes. Who were the few special people in your past that expected greatness from you, challenged you, supported you, and helped you become the person you are today? These were your coaches. You may not have called them by that name but I'll bet that you'll recognize them repeatedly as you read about the traits and behaviors that make a great coach.

There are many important skills that leaders wanting to coach need to develop. Listening, giving feedback, and performance planning are high on this list. *Unleashed!* does not teach you any of these skills. Instead, this book seeks only to remind you of the distinctive qualities and timeless practices of the great coach ... and then challenges you to be this kind of person and employ these practices in your leadership role.

In this book, you will be invited to answer the three crucial questions every leader must address before setting out to coach:

1. Have you earned the right to coach?
2. Are you capable of establishing the kind of relationship necessary for coaching?
3. Are you willing to engage in the kind of conversation that stimulates changes in performance?

These questions form the foundation of the Great Expectations model of coaching. This universal model has long been used by professional coaches and managers alike to produce remarkable results and I'm delighted to share it with you. Just as my mother found exceptional ability in an ordinary boy, the Great Expectations model will help you unleash the hidden talents of the people you coach!

Part 1

EXPECTING GREATNESS

"All that there is to the making of a successful, happy, and beautiful life, is the knowledge and application of simple, root principles."

James Allen

It appears that most of us seek greatness in some form. Ask anyone to tell you about their ambitions and you will often hear this adjective used to describe all sorts of aspirations. We want to become "a great father," "a great manager," "a great runner," or "a great pianist." The pursuit of greatness is probably closely connected with the most fundamental human needs.

Reminding others of the pursuit of their individual greatness may be one of the most important roles of those who seek to teach. On the occasion of Winston Churchill's death in 1965, the political philosopher, Leo Strauss, told his students that "we have no higher duty, and no more pressing duty, than to remind ourselves and our students, of political greatness, of human greatness, of the peaks of human excellence. For we are supposed to train ourselves and others in seeing things as they are, and this means above all in seeing their greatness and their misery, their excellence and their vileness, their nobility and their triumphs ..."

During the past couple of decades I have had the opportunity to observe scores of organizational teams in action. I have seen all kinds of teams ranging from those that were highly effective to those that were completely dysfunctional. Much has been written about the characteristics of high performing teams with authors attributing factors such as shared values, speedy conflict resolution, reliable communication processes and good interpersonal skills to the success of these teams. I disagree. I simply have not seen any of these traits *universally* present in the successful teams I have encountered. In fact, I have seen very effective teams in which the members had widely diverse values, extensive conflict, poor communication processes and lousy interpersonal skills. The only feature that these teams had in common was high expectations. They expected greatness from themselves and each other. Encana, a large Canadian oil and gas producer, recognizes this and has embeded the idea in its corporate constitution by explicitly stating that "We have great expectations of one another. Living up to them will enable us to experience the thrill and fulfillment of being part of a successful team and the pride of building a great company." They recognize the power of expecting greatness.

1

The Leader as Coach

"You cannot teach a man anything. You can only help him discover it within himself."

Galileo

■ have four things to say right up front.

First, leading today's organizations is difficult work. Organizations are chaotic, demanding, and messy. As Clarke and Crossland state in their book, *The Leader's Voice:*

> "You will certainly stumble. Failure will stalk you like a predator. The toughest problems will be yours alone. You must take responsibility for the failures and give credit for the successes. Lose the fantasy that you will be cherished, immortalized and revered. Expect long hours and few moments of gratitude."

If the raw, unvarnished honesty of this quote has you nodding your head, read on, because you get it! Leadership is difficult. Coaching is tougher!

Secondly, there's no simple, multi-step coaching process that you can follow to become a great coach (or leader for that matter). Coaching is a way of *being,* not doing. Despite what many authors will have you believe, there is no universal formula for coaching—it's far too big an endeavor to be compressed into a finite number of steps. Coaching is a complex human-to-human process that needs to be adapted to the countless different ways that humans interact with and respond to one another—much to the frustration of those who set out to coach!

Thirdly, you have to change. I wish I could give you better news, but I cannot. You *must* change. Being a great coach is primarily about who *you* are in your relationships with other people. Think for a moment about your staff, co-workers, boss, and customers. Think about your interactions with them, about your influence on them, and the impact you have on their working lives. Are you important to them? Do they perform better because of their relationship with you? Would others call you a coach? Do the people with whom you interact trust that you have their best interests at heart? Do others attribute their success to you? If you continue following the same course, you will keep getting the same results—or lack of results—you are getting now. Are you happy with these results? No? So a change is required. Since who you are with others is the key factor in determining your ability to coach others for high performance, the change must start with you.

And lastly, at least half of the people who work on your team or in your organization consider themselves "not engaged." Recent Gallup surveys report that approximately 70 percent of respondents admit that they are not performing anywhere near their full potential.[1] Face it. Some of these people work for you, and they are leaving their best talents and efforts at the front door every morning. It's easy to look around our organizations and spot the very poor performers. You know the ones: bad attitudes, minimal production, and little initiative. But what about those in your organization who are performing well enough, but nowhere near their full potential? How many people on your team fall into this category? Worse, might there be some whom you believe are fully engaged, but who are actually only performing just well enough to get the job done? What if your top performers have talents that are never used? What if your poorer performers are really able to contribute at much higher levels? It is tempting to attribute those depressing Gallup statistics to other teams and other organizations, and not our own. But this disengagement has to be happening somewhere and it is likely occurring in the building you walk into each day.

Take a long, hard look at yourself as a leader. What do you see? Is it time to change? Are you ready to be a different leader? Are you ready to be a coach?

If you answered yes, you are now likely wondering how to increase your coaching effectiveness. Think back for a moment on your own career. Can you identify a person who saw talents and potential in you that no one else did? Someone who encouraged you to explore new possibilities? Someone who challenged you to achieve a higher level of performance? A person who truly cared about your development and suc-

cess, and invested those rarest of commodities in you: time and attention? Why does this particular person come to mind? What did this person do to make such an impact on you? What personal qualities attract-
ed you? How did you feel about yourself in her presence? Is there
something she said or did that you remember to this day because it had
such a positive effect on the person you have become? I have just introduced you to an outstanding coach.

Can you be this person in the lives of others? If so, are you prepared
to make fundamental changes in the way you lead in order to be such an
important individual in the lives and careers of others?

As a manager, you're ideally positioned to play the role of coach. In
fact, because there are so few good coaches in the workplace, by becoming a great coach you can distinguish yourself as one of the most integral
types of leaders—the developer of talent. The opportunity awaits you but
it is not easy. You likely already have solid interpersonal and leadership
skills; most managers these days are astute enough to develop these
early in their careers. But while they are without a doubt important, they
are not the subject of this book. The Great Expectations model of coaching consists of universal, timeless principles that will help you move from
simply being a good leader to being the kind of person whom others readily invite into conversations about some of the most important, and often
most highly guarded, spaces of their lives—conversations about their talents, aspirations, and potential.

This model is about high-level, one-on-one communication between
you, the **Leader Coach**, and the individual you coach, the **Talent**. In
Unleashed!, we refer to the person receiving coaching as the Talent in
recognition of the natural abilities he possesses. Our job as coaches is to
challenge him to fully employ all his gifts and to unleash his highest performance. This book will not teach you how to *do* coaching; coaching is
not something that can be *done to* someone. Instead, it challenges you to
establish the kind of relationships that facilitate real performance improvement, and to engage in conversations that inspire others to achieve their
full potential. It takes you beyond the mechanics of the coaching process
to address not so much what you *do* in the role of coach, but rather who
you *are* in the role of coach.

Defining High Performance

Early in my career, I had the good fortune of working with Dr. Herb
Shepard who taught me to see high performance in people as a direction,

not a destination. As a young technologist, I had spent the first few years of my career eagerly measuring the performance of all manner of things —processes, systems, machines, and people—treating them all essentially the same. Through many conversations and much coaching, Herb encouraged me to see human performance in a new light. "Do you really believe that humans were created to be judged on the same scale as machines?" he would ask. One day Herb handed me a book entitled *Born to Win* by Muriel James and Dorothy Jongeward. I read the first page and I was thunderstruck by the boldness and clarity of the authors' view on this matter.

> "Each human being is born as something new, something that never existed before. ... Each person has a unique way of seeing, hearing, touching, tasting, and thinking. Each has his or her own unique potential—capabilities and limitations. Each can be a significant, thinking, aware, and creative being—a productive person, a winner."

So what is high performance? If we are to coach for it, we must be able to describe it. Many organizations invest heavily in both defining and measuring individual performance. Job descriptions, annual reviews, 360 assessments, competency lists, and MBOs are examples of processes commonly used by organizations in their attempt to calibrate individual performance. To the coach, however, defining and measuring high performance is quite simple; it is not an achievement but a journey. It's realized when the Talent is on the road towards fully utilizing his natural capabilities in his work (and everywhere else in his life, for that matter). The Leader Coach's role is to help the Talent onto this road and help him accelerate his journey. And who determines if the Talent is performing at a high level? The Talent—much to the consternation of performance assessment proponents everywhere.

You Are the Instrument

Like it or not, you are always on display. As someone in a leadership role, the impact of your actions is noted and magnified. Your behavior is continually scrutinized. People watch you and form opinions about who you really are. They even make up stories about you when they do not have enough information to paint a complete picture. They're not being intentionally judgmental; they are just fulfilling the human need to have a frame of reference when dealing with you. They ask themselves if you're the kind of person they respect and trust. Is he the kind of person I want poking around in some of the most sensitive and important areas of my performance and career? Do I trust and respect him enough to believe that he has value to offer me in my role? Will he truly have my best interests at heart?

Do you inspire the trust necessary for others to want to share their most daunting problems and ardent dreams with you? You may have a desire to coach, but the decision to coach is not yours alone. Coaching cannot happen unless another person invites you in to do so. Coaching will *not* happen until you've earned the right to make it happen.

> *"Who you are speaks so loudly, I can't hear what you are saying."*
>
> Ralph Waldo Emerson

> *"Leadership is more about who you are as a human being than what you do for a living. It's more about being than doing. If we don't have a deep soul and a deep sense of ourselves as we engage with the world, leadership becomes manipulative: How can I get you to do what I want you to do and have you feel good about it?"*
>
> Dr. Robert Terry,
> *President of the Terry Group*

> *"Healthy leaders are ... very talented in self-observation and self-analysis; the best leaders are highly motivated to spend time in self-reflection."*
>
> Manfred F. R. Kets De Vries

> *"Coaching people to unleash their aspirations, move beyond what they already think and know, and maximize their results is one of the highest aspirations of what it is to be human."*
>
> Robert Hargrove,
> *Masterful Coaching Fieldbook*

Whenever I want to coach others to higher levels of performance, I have to begin by looking at my own performance. This is the first—somewhat annoying—prerequisite of coaching! It would be so much easier if all I had to do was talk about higher levels of performance for others. But we are all pretty transparent, and we can expect to have little coaching impact unless it is obvious to others that we hold ourselves to the same high standard of performance. It's pretty tough to fake this. When I enter a coaching relationship, I have to remind myself that great coaching starts with me. It is an inside-out game, so I need to start by focusing on my own work.

How do you become a great coach? It depends. Some aspects of coaching will come naturally to you while others will need to be developed. Fortunately, coaching is an observable, learnable set of practices and approaches and *everybody* can do it. I have never met a person who could not employ her unique set of talents and aptitudes in the service of another. Coaching is less about having specific abilities and talents than it is about *choosing* to be coach-like.

Managers who seek to become coaches are well advised to look beyond their usual repertoire of leadership skills in their search for coaching effectiveness. Those who have become great coaches have combined their natural leadership strengths with two key practices employed by professional coaches:

1. They establish potent, development-focused relationships, and

2. They engage in difficult, performance-changing conversations.

The coaching relationship is at once dangerous and challenging, caring, and supportive. As a coach, you don't tell the Talent what to do, nor do you merely listen. Your job is much more complicated. The Leader Coach needs to help the Talent see her very best abilities, confront her with her own aspirations, and challenge her to perform to her highest potential.

It is interesting how much time and effort organizations invest in the performance appraisal process yet how little evidence exists to support its effectiveness. Can you honestly recall a pivotal change in your performance or career that was the result of a performance appraisal? Did the feedback you received from a supervisor during a performance appraisal ever inspire you to change the way you function in the organization? Have you ever received a rating that was the motivation to achieve the position you have today? Maybe, but it's unlikely. I have posed these questions to hundreds of leaders and the implication usually stops them cold. They can rarely recall even a single instance when a performance appraisal had a significant influence on their performance or career. Their response, however, is quite a bit different when I ask them to name individuals who *have* influenced their careers. Most have little difficulty identifying two or three people who have been the stimulus for career-changing and sometimes life-changing decisions.

Would you like to be known as a leader who routinely has a profound impact on the careers and lives of others or merely as a manager who gets the job done? Do you want to leave a real legacy in the form of unleashed talent or just have a fine reputation as a solid manager? The Great Expectations model of coaching is about leaving a permanent, positive mark in the lives of the people around you. It's about making a real and lasting contribution. It's about your legacy.

The big question is, "Are you up to it?" Are you prepared to commit yourself to the success of another? Can you see your role through entirely different eyes? Can you function as a guide rather than a supervisor, a catalyst rather than a counselor, a facilitator rather than an advisor? What are you prepared to sacrifice to become a coach?

2

The Power of
Great Expectations

"Through appreciating every aspect of human life, we can benefit others."

Sakong Mipham,
Turning the Mind into an Alley

The Expectation/Performance Connection

Consider for a moment the people with whom you work most closely. Who would you classify as your A players? And your B players? What distinguishes these groups from one another? What characteristics are shared by the A players? What do the B players have in common? What thoughts do you have most frequently about each group?

Now consider this: they know how you rate them.

People are remarkably perceptive. Whether you express your assessments verbally or not, the people on your team have a pretty good idea into which category you've placed them. We communicate our opinions quite clearly, often unconsciously, through a variety of verbal and non-verbal cues. We change the tone of our voice depending on whom we are addressing. We avoid eye contact with some while granting others our full attention. More often than not, the people around us know what we think of them, and—here is the crux of coaching—**people live up, or down, to our expectations of them.**

We communicate these high or low expectations in many ways. We give more time and attention to those perceived as high performers and less to those we see as low performers. We smile more often with those we think well of, less with those we do not. Next time you are in a meeting, notice with whom you seek or avoid eye contact. We tend to call upon those we consider low performers less often than we do high performers, even granting concessions to high performers that we do not to give low performers. We criticize low performers more frequently than high performers. We praise low performers for mediocre results, reinforcing low standards instead of demanding better. We provide less coaching and direction for weaker performers, demand less work and effort from them than we would from those we consider strong performers. The list goes on.

The expectations we hold for others are a direct predictor of their performance. And it's not because we are such excellent judges of character. In reality, it's because the opinions we have of others are self-fulfilling prophecies. No matter how they are manifested, the cues you send are expressions of your thoughts and expectations, and they have an enormous impact on everyone around you. As a leader in the workplace, your colleagues pick up these subtle signals and respond by adjusting their behavior in accordance with your assumptions about them and their abilities. Here's the point: by expecting less-than-greatness from those with whom you work, you are actually contributing to the less-than-great results.

Research conducted by psychologist Robert Rosenthal into how teachers' expectations affect student performance confirms what I have experienced in my own work with leadership training. In the Oak School Experiment, teachers were told that a group of students had been specially tested and had been identified as intellectual bloomers. They were told that although the students might start out slowly, they were expected to show above-average gains over the course of the school year. At the end of the year, these so-called bloomers had done just that: they showed a significant jump both in IQ scores and overall academic achievement. Their teachers also reported that these particular students were more friendly, outgoing, and eager to learn than their peers. The truth, however, was that the students identified as intellectual bloomers had actually been randomly selected from the class list. Nothing distinguished them from their peers except their teacher's expectations.[2]

The Rosenthal study is not alone in its conclusions. In his book *Self-Fulfilling Prophecy,* Professor Robert Tauber presents the results of over 700 doctoral dissertations and countless journal articles on stereotyping and the use of social locators, such as race, gender, ethnicity, physical appearance, age, socioeconomic status, and special needs. He found that, even in scientifically conducted studies, "what we expect, all too often, is exactly what we get."[3]

What does this mean for the Leader Coach? Simply this: your assessment of others matters. People know what you think of them and they respond accordingly. When you think of others as unmotivated, incompetent, or unintelligent, they know it and resent it. When you think of others as unique, talented, and developing, they know this as well and respond accordingly. By seeing people at their very best, the Leader Coach sets the stage for high performance.

> "We can sense how others are feeling towards us. Given a little time, we can always tell when we're being coped with, manipulated, beneath veneers of niceness. And we typically resent it ... What we'll know and respond to is how that person is regarding us ... we can tell how other people feel about us, and it's to that that we respond."
>
> The Arbinger Institute

❋ TRY THIS

Analyze **others'** behavior as you do your own. For example, when another person is late, attribute it first to the incredible demands on their time rather than their disrespect for your time. When your waiter screws up your lunch order, attribute it to the possibility that the kitchen recently lost a staff member and is struggling to meet demands, not that the waiter is being incompetent. For a week, find ten opportunities a day to practice this. At the end of the week ask yourself one question: Why are others relating well to me this week?

The Halo Effect and the Horn Effect

Researchers have identified two patterns in the way people assess the overall ability of others. The Halo Effect describes the tendency for one good characteristic to dictate the overall opinion of an individual. When a person demonstrates exceptional ability in one area, we are more willing to see his gifts and talents in other arenas as well. For example, when looking at a very attractive person, we might assume that he is talented and easy to work with in a professional environment.

Forming opinions about people in this manner has a negative impact on all areas of management. Managers may allow a strong rating in one area to influence their overall rating of a staff member. As a result, favored people fail to get constructive commentary on the full spectrum of their performance, while others go unrecognized for their contributions. One part of their team is not asked to perform any higher than the bare minimum needed for success to be acknowledged, while the other part is given little incentive to achieve more because their current contributions are largely overlooked. The overall effect: a team that performs no better than it absolutely has to—hardly a recipe for great success.

The converse of the Halo Effect is the Horn Effect. This phenomenon receives less attention than its corollary but it has just as much of an impact. When a person seems deficient in one critical area, his manager often assumes he is deficient in other ways too. These skills may have little or no bearing on one another, but the manager's mind makes the leap from not-good-at-one-thing to not-good-at-many-things.

For a moment, consider your own shortcomings. Now imagine that someone focused only on those aspects of your performance, continually pointing out the ways in which you are lacking. What if your manager judged your entire value as a team member solely on those things you failed to do well? How inspired would you be to achieve? Most people do not get inspired by talking about their weaknesses, failures, mistakes, and flaws.

Now, imagine having great expectations of all your staff. Coaching for high performance means challenging each individual to perform at a higher level—regardless of how well or poorly he has been doing up until now. Coaching for high performance is applicable to everyone. People want to be successful, important, and engaged, and to know that their work matters. What if you saw everyone as a unique person with individual hopes and dreams? Most certainly there are people in your organization with latent talents that are waiting to be discovered and applied. What if, instead of assessing performance, you spent your time and energy seeking out these exiled talents and helping to unleash their potential?

> *"Be kind. Everyone you meet is fighting a hard battle."*
>
> T.H. Thompson

The Coaching Perspective

Take a moment to consider the people with whom you work most closely. Try to see them not as high performers and low performers, but rather as individuals with wonderfully wide-ranging personalities, talents, and abilities. For most of us this is not easy because we are so practiced at rating others on many scales such as likeability, intelligence, trustworthiness, and commitment. Can you suspend these ratings, if only temporarily, and truly look at these individuals through softer eyes that see only the greatness in others? This Coaching Perspective forms the foundation of the Great Expectations model. This does not mean that you need to condone poor performance but rather that you will choose to see it as unused potential. Until you are able to see others through this perspective, you cannot be an effective coach.

A friend of mine, Scott, learned the power of perspective early in his career. As a young man, he spent a year in Micronesia assisting with the development of the local school system. On one occasion, he was sent on an assignment to a remote island in the company of a local student— a sixteen-year-old boy who was quite pleasant, but who, according to the teachers, was not very bright and showed little academic promise. It was a long trip, and by the time they reached their destination, both Scott and his companion were hungry. This was a small village, with no place to purchase supper, so the young man took Scott on a mile-long walk across the tidal flats in search of food. Before long, this young man had served him an impressive five-course meal, including salad and dessert, straight from the ocean. Scott was amazed. Here was this boy who, in Scott's words, "was considered not very intelligent by many of the Western teachers because he struggled with reading and writing … but had this amazing ability to thrive in nature!" This incident has served as a powerful reminder to Scott that assessing others is really quite futile and that it is much more fruitful to spend one's energies seeking out the best in them. This boy had enormous abilities which would leave most of us in awe if we allowed ourselves to recognize them. Once Scott took away the filter of Western educational success, he was able to see this boy's abilities for what they truly were.

When we adopt the Coaching Perspective, for a period of time we must suspend our judgments. I'm not asking you to stop judging people altogether—that would be virtually impossible. Judgment is a natural human behavior; it is how we understand and navigate the world around us. We meet new people and have what we call, unglamorously, a gut reaction about who they are, and instinctively determine where they fit into our personal hierarchies. We quickly decide how much we can trust others, or how valuable they might be to us, or how much potential they have. Even when we experience people in just one setting, our minds quickly fill in the unknowns. They are smart or dull, motivated or lazy, engaged or disengaged, interesting or boring, trustworthy or dangerous. This human tendency to judge can be useful: it helps us make sense of a chaotic world and make decisions about how we should interact with others. However, it also means that at times we don't assess accurately; we misinterpret and we overlook. The discipline of coaching demands that, in the moment, we cast aside this compelling instinct to label and judge. The Coaching Perspective challenges us to consider the questions: What if we are completely wrong about a person? What if he is *not* who we think he is? What if he has an entirely different set of motives, values and traits? Because one thing is absolutely clear—whatever we think of this person—we are wrong.

Allowing yourself to take a new perspective on the people around you has a transformative effect on relationships. Can you start with a blank slate and approach another without preconceived ideas? Can you forget who you think he is or what you think is possible for him? I know it's hard. As one of my clients recently exclaimed, "But it isn't just me, the whole department knows this person is *that* way!" Yes, and the whole department is probably wrong too. Just as individuals use judgments to understand the world around them, so too do groups collectively make up stories which help them to make better sense out of the inexplicable entities called people.

The Coaching Perspective does not come naturally. It's a discipline that needs to be intentionally adopted and rigorously practiced. It starts with seeing people as empty canvases ready to be filled with wondrous colors. Most of us credit ourselves with an open mind; coaching gives us the opportunity to prove it.

As an organizational leader, no doubt you've taken this perspective many times. This is not new to you. Coaching simply asks that you take this perspective more intentionally. Coaching is both a process and a discipline. Regardless of your personal feelings for the person you coach, adopting this perspective with *anyone* is a choice you will need to make.

The "L" Word

A workshop participant once asked me if I like all of my coaching clients. The question caught me off guard and in a moment of candor I told the participant that, while I do not always like my clients, I always love them in the moment. Seeing several looks of astonishment in the classroom, I went on to say that I rarely disliked a client, but some would not fall into the category of people that I would naturally like. I'm no Will Rogers; there are people I don't like. My critical nature leads me to make judgments about people, their personalities, their values, and their motives. I truly strive to *not* make these judgments but, being human, I am not always successful.

Being a product of large business organizations and hoping that this book will find its way into these same organizations, I tried to find a way around using the "L" word but failed. There is simply no other way to describe how I feel about my client in the coaching relationship. I can only approach my clients with a coach's perspective if I can love them. Strange as it may seem, I do not have to like them. I do not have to form life-long friendships with them. But in the moment when I enter a relationship to discuss their aspirations and their future, I must love them. There is no other way for me to put aside my judgments and to see them at their best.

Surprisingly, we will also not always like our coaches. It is not the coach's job to befriend us but rather to challenge us to perform at our very best and to facilitate our efforts to do so. Jim, a successful software executive and entrepreneur, attributes much of his professional success to Mr. Davidge, his eighth grade English teacher—a man he found overbearing and impersonal. Jim describes Mr. Davidge as a tough, single-minded teacher who made it his mission to equip his students with the high-level grammar skills that he believed were the underpinning of all other learning in life. He had an uncompromising belief that the most important thing one could learn in the school system was the English language, and was unrelenting in demanding an outstanding command of grammar from all of his students. Mr. Davidge often said, "You have got to get the carpet correct. Worry about the fringe later." He would accept nothing less than excellent work from his students and they knew it. In Jim's words, "He was relentless." Jim is fond of saying that he never studied grammar after that year with Mr. Davidge because he had nothing more to learn. Looking back over his career, Jim recognizes the foundation that was laid during his eighth grade. To this day he thanks Mr. Davidge for the unique joy he still gets from the study of English grammar and believes that it has fueled both his leadership communication skills as well as his passion for great literature.

Somewhat ironically, assuming the Coaching Perspective gives you much more than you give away. When I can truly approach my clients from this perspective, I learn much more from them than they learn from me. I am always inspired by the courage they display as they struggle with their unique challenges. Focusing on the development of another and watching that person reach new heights of performance is a reward like no other. And seeing that person go on to coach and develop others—this is the big payoff of coaching!

"What we are seeking ... is the rapture of being alive."

Joseph Campbell

3

The Great
Expectations Model

"Treat people as if they were what they ought to be and you help them to become what they are capable of being."

Johann W. von Goethe

The great coach *deliberately* seeks out others' highest potential, often intentionally overlooking their shortcomings in the process. For many of us, this practice does not come naturally. In fact, the contrary is more often true; it is finding fault that comes most naturally. We need only look to the media to view this tendency at a systemic level. Turn on the news and what do you see? Everything that went wrong today: the accidents, the killings, the government follies and scandals. Basically, anything that stood out negatively. Among the hundreds of planes that took off and landed on time, we hear about the one that did not.

We like to expect things to go as planned—that is why we are often frustrated when they do not. As the Buddhist saying goes, "Our only problem is that we want not to have any problems." As a result, when problems occur, they stand out so we notice them more. However, our trouble begins when we focus on them, talk about them, and report on them. This is where our critical nature is fatally flawed. When we do this often enough, our world becomes filled with only those things that went wrong; all the mistakes and all of the things that should have gone differently become our focus. This is an unfortunate place to direct our most important commodity, our attention. But because most people do this, we fail to notice that it's happening. It has become pervasive. Because it's almost universally adopted, this skewed perspective is considered normal. In the words of internationally renowned psychologist Erich Fromm, "That millions share the same forms of mental pathology does not make those people sane."

Our critical tendency, however, is not inherently negative—the skill of noticing what is missing can be very useful if it is properly employed. The ability to see where there is room for improvement is the essence of our problem-solving abilities. Our habit, however, tends to be to identify *people*, rather than actions or behaviors, and our response to them as the source of the problem. Such fault finding tends to not be an effective way of interacting with other human beings (let alone a joyful way to live).

As a leader and a coach, this is exciting news!

With countless people today focused on what is *missing* from any given situation, and unwilling to look at ways to fill the gaps, there is great opportunity to stand out as someone who is a pioneer for positive change. You can be the one who focuses on everything that is right or at least the person who focuses on how to turn a challenge into an opportunity. Focus on the best in others. Highlight the great things they do everyday. Ask yourself how you can help your colleagues reach their highest visions of success. Care about other people as human beings. Genuinely seek to be of service to those with whom you interact. Confront others with their potential and have the courage to challenge them to live up to that potential. Tell others the absolute truth about their performance. That is the essence of high performance coaching. Naïve? Unrealistic? I don't think so. *Unleashed!* is certainly about being an exceptional leader. It's about doing something different, something as straightforward as focusing solely on another's talents, something as naïve as believing we can all pursue our highest potential, something as odd as genuinely caring about another's success as much as your own.

If you are willing to embrace this one simple yet powerful philosophy, you will touch people in a profound and meaningful way. Great coaches are *intentional* in the way they interact with others. This discipline becomes a habit of the Leader Coach.

What would it take for you to develop the habit of focusing on only the best in others?

It is imperative that you see your role not as a judge of others' performance but rather as an advocate for their potential. Great coaches expect others to bring all of their talents and energies to every job. They expect others to do their best work. To this end, the great coach confronts others with their own highest aspirations and talents, and in so doing, advances them towards achieving their version of success. The leverage point of coaching is this—figure out what another person most wants and become an advocate for them achieving it.

Walking our Walk

Marcus Buckingham, a best-selling author and former Senior Researcher at the Gallup Organization, has said that "the best strategy for building a competitive organization is to help individuals become more of who they are."[4] And yet many of us continue to leave a large part of ourselves behind each day as we walk into our organizations. And many of us fail to truly recognize and celebrate others for who they really are.

> "The great teachers of my life gave me a precious gift. It was not a tool, process, or technology; it was something deeper and more profound. They helped me understand that what really matters when helping people or organizations through change and transition is not technique but authenticity, vulnerability, and empathy. They taught me that connecting with others at the warm, messy, and unscientific level of the human spirit is a prerequisite for any methodology or process."

> David M. Noer,
> *Learning Journeys*

The process of successful coaching involves much more than just talking with others about their goals and dreams. While rich dialogue can uncover new ideas and generate innovative solutions, this kind of interaction alone is not coaching. Where dialogue pursues new ideas, coaching pursues entirely new attitudes and behaviors. Dialogue is the talk, coaching is the walk.

It takes a special person to focus on another's career and aspirations, but that's exactly what a great coach does. She does not feel the need to impress, nor does she even need to feel that her coaching was of significant value to the Talent. The best coaches have a clear appreciation of their own gifts and talents. They don't need to feed their egos by showing the Talent how smart they are. This is noteworthy because all too often new coaches will subtly make the coaching about them, looking for the Talent to affirm their value as a coach. Unintentionally, they change the topic of conversation and make it about *their* need to be helpful. True coaching is focused solely on another. Everything said or done is in answer to the question, "What do I need to do or say (or *not* do or say) right now in order to help this person achieve their version of success?"

When I look back at my own career, I am in awe of the selflessness of my own personal coaches. I readily recall several memorable conversations

—two or three key sentences that forever changed the way I saw myself: my mother, who told me I was smart and would therefore need to help others to learn; my first boss, who said that I was the finest cherry picker in the whole orchard; my dear friend and business partner, the late Boyd Clarke, who said, "some people are harder to love than others but it is your job to love them anyway." This is the power of coaching: a single penetrating sentence spoken by a person who cares deeply about another's success.

The Great Expectations model of high performance coaching introduces organizational leaders to the best practices employed by professional coaches. There is nothing mysterious or mystical about them. But while these basic principles of Great Expectations are simple and straightforward, the difficulty lies in the consistency and depth of their application. Great Expectations coaching calls for a considerable personal investment on the part of the coach.

Earning Your Demotion

As a manager in one of today's organizations, you are probably well-equipped with a toolbox of solid skills for handling performance discussions such as giving feedback and engaging in active listening. But the Great Expectations model challenges you to do more than practice these same management practices. As a Leader Coach, your role is to engage people in a new and special kind of relationship, a relationship that requires you to become a peer of the Talent, if only temporarily. This enables a fundamentally different kind of conversation, one in which you are actually welcomed by the Talent as an equal and accepted as a Leader Coach. Coaching from a position of "I know the answers and will advise or tell you what to do" simply does not work. In order to coach, the Talent has to see you as a fellow human being rather than a superior within the organization. Put bluntly—you must earn a demotion in her eyes (see Part Three: A Perfect Partnership).

The Great Expectations Model

Reading this, you may feel a little overwhelmed by the magnitude of your role as a developer of talent. It's understandable; it takes a major commitment to put yourself into the service of another. Do not be deterred! This is important work, possibly your most important work. The Great Expectations model is based on easy-to-understand coaching concepts and, most encouraging, generates immediate results. It incorporates practices and tools from several highly regarded schools of thought in leadership and organizational development, and blends the best of these together into a single powerful model. It is simple, straightforward and effective, and any manager, from supervisor to CEO, can use it to create a culture of high performance.

The Great Expectations model of high performance coaching consists of three guiding principles. They are not predetermined coaching steps. They are three interdependent principles which operate concurrently, each representing a key element that exists within all effective coaching relationships. They are:

⇨ Earning the Right to Coach

⇨ A Perfect Partnership

⇨ Dangerous Conversations

The Great Expectations Model of Coaching

Earning the Right to Coach

Managers are not automatically coaches. Hiring, planning, performance management and other such tasks naturally accompany the role of manager—but coaching does not. We do not assume the mantle of coach just because we are managers. Becoming a Leader Coach requires that two choices be made: the first is our decision to help another person create personal change, and the second is the choice another person makes to include you in his effort to change.

Again, coaching is not something we do *to* another person. It is a peer-to-peer relationship in which the Leader Coach is welcomed into a personal, behavior-changing relationship. Managers must *earn* this welcome. And they can do so by knowing and living their most important values **(authenticity)**, by being fully aware of their unique strengths and gifts **(self-esteem)**, and by having a genuine interest in the success of the Talent **(noble intention)**.

❊ EARNING THE RIGHT TO COACH

1. Authenticity
2. Self-esteem
3. Noble Intention

A Perfect Partnership

We call the high performance coaching relationship "a perfect partnership" to signify the exceptional character of this performance-altering association. This is a unique and special relationship, in which the Talent is **appreciated** at his best, **confronted** with his own talents and aspirations, and held **accountable** to live up to his own highest standards.

❊ A PERFECT PARTNERSHIP

1. Appreciation
2. Confrontation
3. Accountability

Dangerous Conversations

The Great Expectations model challenges Leader Coaches to engage in an intense form of dialogue we call *Dangerous Conversations.* Most on-the-job conversations involve the exchange of information—instructions, advice, and opinions—and have relatively predictable outcomes. Dangerous conversations are significantly different in that they are inherently uncertain and risky. Their outcomes are unknown. They take us outside our comfort zones and challenge us to consider new perspectives. The dangerous conversation is a wide-ranging exchange between the Leader Coach and the Talent exploring aspirations, values, and the current situation; taking its participants to new depths **(discovery)**; generating new possibilities, opportunities, and perspectives **(creation)**; and forging new action plans and accountabilities **(commitment)**.

❋ DANGEROUS CONVERSATIONS

1. Discovery
2. Creation
3. Commitment

Superior coaching and remarkable success for your organization are only a few steps away! When you routinely employ the three enduring principles of the Great Expectations Model in your one-on-one leadership, their effect will be transformative.

EARNING THE RIGHT
TO COACH

> *"First one must change. I first watch myself, check myself, and then expect changes from others."*
>
> Dalai Lama XIV

First, Coach Yourself

The Great Expectations coaching model is designed to help you become a coach to the most important Talent of all—Yourself. It's only when you can effectively manage, motivate, and coach yourself that you know how to most effectively manage, motivate, and coach others to achieve greater levels of performance. If leadership is about going first, as a Leader Coach you must first strive to live up to *your own* fullest potential. This is what is meant by "Earning the Right to Coach."

As the Leader Coach, you are the instrument of change. Who you are will have more of an effect on your ability to facilitate exceptional performance in others than any theory or technique I could ever impart to you. It will be through your own actions, attitudes, and character that others will identify you as someone they want to be coached by. You are the ultimate coaching tool and no book or manual will ever take precedence over your own personal presence. This is why Earning the Right To Coach is the top ring of the Great Expectations model; everything else flows from it.

What have I learned from my own best coaches? How did they earn the right to coach me? The people from whom I have sought, and continue to seek, coaching are clear about their personal values and live them consistently. First and foremost, they are **authentic**. My own great coaches also had a high level of **self-esteem**—one of the reasons they were able to engage authentically with me was that they did not need to work out their own issues at my expense. Finally, my own best coaches were people who entered into our relationship with **noble intentions**. These were people who genuinely cared about *my* success.

> *"If you wish to be a leader, you will be frustrated, for very few people wish to be led. If you aim to be a servant, you will never be frustrated."*
>
> Frank F. Warren

You already possess your greatest resource as a coach. It's within you. Your ability to relate to others is inextricably linked to your own self-knowledge. What do *you* value most? What unique gifts and talents do *you* bring to people and situations? What part of your work do you most love? What part do you dislike? What are your assumptions about those with whom you work most closely? What thoughts do you think most often when you reflect on your department and your company? Take a moment to contemplate these and be completely honest. The answers to these questions are already being broadcast to everyone with whom you interact. Either overtly or covertly, you communicate these things before you've even spoken a word! Try to step outside of yourself and answer these questions:

⇨ What impact—positive, negative, or otherwise—do you have on those with whom you work most closely? To what extent do you think others would agree with your assessment of your impact?

⇨ What would it be like to work with someone like you? Would you feel valued, appreciated, talented, heard, and valued as a team member? Why or why not?

⇨ Is being in your presence a positive experience or do you worry that people feel better when you are not there? If so, why?

Be gentle and appreciative in this self-reflection. Self-analysis without compassion is rarely useful. Remember, you are doing this personal work so that you can help others ask these same questions of themselves with the same level of courage, honesty, and compassion.

To Earn the Right to Coach, it is essential that you, as the Leader Coach, begin by assessing your own readiness. Using this assessment, you can focus on your own development plan—the one that will require more of *you.* By continuing to develop yourself, you *earn the right* to challenge others to embark on their own journey of self-development.

> *"It is only when the teacher has the internal confidence of knowing that he is living what he is trying to teach that the student can hear the teaching."*

Jonathon Flaum

4

Authenticity

"That inner voice has both gentleness and clarity. So to get to authenticity, you really keep going down to the bone, to the honesty, and the inevitability of something."

Meredith Monk

Are you an authentic leader? I have asked this question of hundreds of managers and usually receive a response such as, "Most certainly, I pride myself on my authenticity." I then ask "Would you rate the managers in your organization who are more senior than you as being as authentic?" Less than fifty percent respond in the affirmative. I then ask them to imagine a scenario in which I bring into the room all of the individuals in their organization who are more junior than they are and ask the same question. They generally concede that this would result in a response nearer to fifty percent than they would like. The consequences for the Leader Coach quickly become apparent. Many, if not most, organization members believe that the majority of leaders in more senior positions are less than completely authentic and, since the Leader Coach is often called upon to coach more junior Talent, odds are the Talent will have initial misgivings regarding the coaching. More simply put, managers are often not trusted largely because they are managers, and they need to find ways to amend this perception early in the coaching relationship.

So what is this attribute called "authenticity?" Terms like honesty, integrity, and genuineness are often given as definitions, but a more compelling description might be created by examining the characteristics and qualities of those leaders you deem authentic. My list is short: just four items, each—as far as I'm concerned—non-negotiable.

If you want to be an authentic leader:

1. Live your values—your principles should be evident in everything you do.
2. Don't equivocate—make your yes mean yes, and your no mean no.
3. Take full accountability for your life—be comfortable saying "I am responsible."
4. If you say it, do it—follow through, even on the small things.

However we define the word, one thing is clear—as a leader in your organization, you are under constant scrutiny, continuously scanned for trustworthiness. Think about how you reacted the last time someone cut you off in traffic. What about the last time you were nearing a critical deadline? How about when you arrived home especially tired after work just to be confronted with a domestic problem? In each of these instances, how did you treat the people around you? What parts of your character were revealed? Stressful situations teach others a lot about who we really are. The Leader Coach recognizes that she is constantly being watched, especially in difficult situations, and is aware that her every action is on display for all to see. Unfortunately, organization leaders often start in the red, mistrusted solely because of their title—all the more reason for a manager to be cognizant of her authenticity.

Authenticity is not a trait that we can claim. We may strive for it, and even practice the necessary disciplines, but it is others who determine if we are authentic. We are or are not authentic only through the eyes of others.

Psychologist Carl Rogers talked about the importance of authenticity during the 1950s in his work on client-centered therapy. He asserted that for a relationship to foster growth and change in an individual, it had to contain what he called "genuineness" as well as "unconditional high regard and empathic understanding." Though Rogers' work pertained specifically to counselor-client therapy, the same principles hold true in the coaching relationship.

Only when the Talent senses that you live your own life with honesty and integrity and that you are bringing that same authenticity to your relationship with him, will you have earned the right to coach. Great coaching relationships are surprisingly straightforward. While actual coaching conversations are far from being predictable, the relationships themselves always sit on foundations of clear, well-articulated values. The Leader Coach provides this foundation.

There is much talk these days about leaders "living their values," but what does this really mean? To the Leader Coach, living one's values means being transparent in the coaching relationship. It means the Talent does not have to guess what's important to you or what your words really mean. Your values are clear, and they influence everything that occurs in the coaching relationship. While great coaches will suspend their immediate needs on behalf of the client (see Chapter 6: Noble Intention), they act and speak from an obvious and distinct value set.

For example, if the Leader Coach places a high value on personal accountability, the Talent will continually be challenged to take full responsibility for her performance. If the Leader Coach values altruism, the Talent will be encouraged to see her work as a contribution to humanity. If innovation is a core value for the Leader Coach, the Talent will be urged to fully develop her natural creative abilities. Each time the Talent interacts with the Leader Coach, she can see evidence of the Leader Coach's values and can rely upon the consistency of these values as she travels along the bumpy road of personal development. The authentic coach provides the foundation needed to navigate this bumpy road.

This does not mean that the Leader Coach requires the Talent to *adopt* his values. It does, however, mean that the Talent knows that the Leader Coach will be honest and consistent. The Leader Coach knows his values and lives them. End of story. The Talent does not even need to *agree* with the values of the Leader Coach; if the Leader Coach lives with his values, he will engender the respect necessary to earn the right to coach another.

To Trust or Not Trust

As human beings, we are hardwired to seek out trustworthiness—or more specifically, untrustworthiness. Without realizing it, we move through our daily lives assessing everyone around us, attempting to detect sincerity and insincerity, and adjusting our behavior accordingly. Before we willingly engage in being coached on something as highly personal as our own performance or career, first we must trust another person enough to thoroughly explore all the important issues related to these subjects, including our dreams, fears, and personal values.

Just How Honest?

Honesty is closely related to trust; it is an essential prerequisite to an effective coaching relationship. But think about it—how often in organizations do we tell only part of the truth (that part of the story that enables us to avoid offending someone or that allows us to skirt the embarrassing issues at hand)? How often do we tell people what we are really thinking, feeling, wanting? Are we are tempted to avoid any truth that makes us uncomfortable?

Is truth an absolute? That is a philosophical point that needs a far more academic forum than this to be properly debated. What I do know is that our ability as human beings to recognize truth and articulate it is neither consistent nor absolute. We can only view the world from our own particular perspective, and when we speak, we do so from that worldview. One way to look at it is that we function within a *range* of honesty. Our conscience takes the liberty of telling us when we have held something back that should have been spoken or when we have lied outright. Of course, honesty is not about saying *everything* that we think, but it is about being true to who we are and sharing what we truly believe. This is much more difficult than it would seem. Honesty begins with us, which begs the questions: How much do I know about myself? How self-aware am I? Am I being honest with myself right now?

Have you ever noticed how some people are so comfortable in their own skin that they can talk about their mistakes quite openly and freely? They embrace their checkered past and view it as a part of the whole journey to personal growth. As coaches, they bring their transparency to the coaching arena and readily earn the Talent's trust because they are honest about who they are. They recognize that it was usually their failures, rather than their successes, that caused their greatest growth. The road may have been bumpy and meandering for them, but they now have a wealth of wisdom to offer and are not plagued with notions of losing face. They are free to be themselves and put their experiences fully at the disposal of the Talent.

> "It is not to our discredit that we have fallen. It is to our credit that we have fallen and gotten back up."
>
> Marianne Williamson,
> *A Return To Love*

Integrity: Values in Action

In their book *The Leadership Challenge,* authors James Kouzes and Barry Posner talk about the overwhelming importance of integrity for leaders. Who do we trust? Without fail, it is those people who we believe have a clear set of values and are firmly committed to living those values in all aspects of their lives. Their actions are consistent and match their words.

We find in them *one* person whom we recognize, whether we meet them at the grocery store, at a Christmas party, or at work. The regular actions and behaviors that we observe in others, over time, become who they are in our eyes.

The flip side: your reputation is comprised of those things you do most frequently, both good and bad. Consider yourself a brand. What would the marketplace say about who you are? What values would they say you demonstrate consistently? Often we will *say* we value certain things like family or health, but when we are honest with ourselves and look at how we actually choose to spend our time, we see that we aren't really living according to our values. Based upon your actual behavior and choices, what would others say you value? Are those the values you want to be known for? Honesty begins when we start accepting who we really are. I am what many call a workaholic. I am always working. I often trade off family for work. This is the truth of who I am. To say otherwise would be to lie to myself, and pretending that my work is a temporary distraction would be categorically untrue. It isn't a distraction. It is my passion and it makes up the majority of my life. I know that about myself, and I don't hide it from anyone, including myself.

> *"The great leaders are those who have come to accept the madness within themselves."*
>
> Mandred F. R. Kets De Vries

It is much easier to *talk* about values and authenticity than actually do something about them. Intellectually, we know authenticity. We recognize authentic people when we see them, and we sense those who are not. Yet how do we bridge the chasm between intellectual knowledge and actually *living* authentic lives? No one can tell you how to be authentic, but they will certainly know, and may even tell you, whether or not you are. Sometimes, you will be the only one who knows when you have sold out your core values or failed to live up to your own standards. You will know when you have not cared well for yourself or respected yourself in relationships with others. Authenticity starts with not letting ourselves down.

To truly be ourselves and put our core values into action in every moment of every day may seem like a goal beyond our reach. Yes, it's hard. Very hard. We live in a world that tries to seduce us into forsaking who we are for who others tell us we should be. Be sexy. Be a consumer. Be tough. Be a winner. The Leader Coach who stands out is the one who is so committed to his values that he is prepared to pay the price for authenticity.

What do I mean by that? Let's say you gave your word and it becomes costly to keep it, either financially or in other ways. You keep it, even if it hurts. If you promised to attend an engagement, and a better, more interesting invitation comes your way, you honor your acceptance of the first event. Keeping your word sounds good, but often times it's not easy. Where are you wrestling with the hard issues to make the hard choices that deep down you know are right? If this is too easy for you, that's a red flag right there. In the movie *A League of their Own,* Jimmy Dugan (played by Tom Hanks) says to a baseball team member, "If it weren't hard, everyone would do it. The hard is what makes it great."

Let's dig a little deeper. Who are you when no one is watching? When the heat is on, when the temptation to compromise on what you believe in is great, what do you choose? Are you prepared to pay the price of authenticity? Or would you rather take the easy way and join the throng who travel the wide highway of playing fast and loose with their values? You'll be as distinctive as a grain of sand at the beach.

In contrast, the Leader Coach stands out in the crowd. She desires to be genuine in all she does. She sets her course and holds it, no matter how the winds of the day blow against her. She bears the marks of authenticity earned over time as she steers faithfully according to those inner values that she knows are right and true for her. Those marks are evident to all around her.

Management guru Tom Peters has said that his definition of a loser is someone who says, "I could have done a lot of cool things if my boss had let me." Indeed. Authenticity is about knowing who we are and living it, regardless of the consequences. And if we look to those leaders who we respect the most, they are very often people who risk much for what they believe. How much are you willing to risk to be seen as an authentic leader? Will you risk being ridiculed? Or looking like a fool? How about risking your job? Every day we have the opportunity to define who we are by taking a stand for our most important values. Most of us are willing to take some risks; the question is how many and for what?

Integrity is not self-righteousness. It's not something for which we seek applause or expect popularity. It is not about comparing ourselves with others nor is it about what others think of us. What really matters is what *we* think of the person we see in the mirror. Every time we fail to live by our own values and highest standards, we chip away at our self-respect. And yet, no matter how often we betray our core values, we can never escape the person in the mirror (though we may give it our best shot!). Like it or not, coaching others to their best performance requires us to expect the best of ourselves as well.

> *"Our deepest calling is to grow into our own authentic self-hood, whether or not it conforms to some image of who we ought to be. As we do so, we will not only find the joy that every human being seeks—we will also find our path of authentic service in the world."*
>
> Parker Palmer,
> *Let Your Life Speak*

5

Self-Esteem

"There is overwhelming evidence that the higher the level of self-esteem, the more likely one will be to treat others with respect, kindness, and generosity

Nathaniel Branden

I have a confession to make: I cannot write. I have been sitting in front of my computer for three hours, my eyes aching, stomach churning, and no words are showing up on the screen. An all-too-familiar voice is screaming in my ear: "You fraud, you imposter! What makes you think anyone would want to read your work? Who cares what you think anyway? What gives you the right to be an author?"

This aggressive, booming voice is responded to by a noticeably meeker, more uncertain one: "But I have years of coaching experience, have received spectacular reviews from The Leader as Coach Workshop, and have written some pretty good stuff before."

The booming voice carries on: "Pure luck," it tells me. "You're just not good enough. The gig is up!"

For many of us, this familiar dialogue plays out all too often. To the coach, these conversations are handcuffs. We all have self-doubt, fearing on some level that we lack the ability to be successful in certain areas of our lives. Even great coaches have these fears. Left unchecked, these conversations severely limit the effect we can have on the development of others. We cannot let the louder voice have the last word. Instead we must recognize it but not allow it to keep us from doing what we know we must do. We need—to paraphrase the title of a popular self-help book—to *hear* the fear and do it anyway.

The point is not to eliminate the voice of self-doubt, but to listen to it, recognize the things it says for the baseless insecurities that they are, and act in spite of it. Great coaches do this because they know that they cannot give away what they do not have; if you cannot move beyond your inner critic, you will have difficulty helping another do so. Similarly, if you do not appreciate yourself, you cannot have appreciation for another. In the words of Thomas S. Szasz,

> *"Self-control and self-esteem vary directly: The more self-esteem a person has, the greater, as a rule, is his desire, and his ability, to control himself. The desire to control others and self-esteem vary inversely: the less self-esteem a person has, the greater, as a rule, is his desire, and his ability, to control others."*[5]

Most of us can identify many very successful people who are lousy coaches. It's not uncommon to find talented people who, because they doubt their personal value, are racked with insecurities. Insecurity generally drives people to try to convince others of their value and worth, often by concealing their failings from public view and relating all their triumphs to everyone who will listen—hoping that if others believe they are successful, eventually they will too. From time to time, we are all guilty of this in some form, whether it's name dropping or directing the conversation to our personal achievements. Self-promotion is not bad in itself, but whenever we do it, others instinctively ask themselves, "What weakness is he trying to cover up?" It's also important that we know when and why we do it. Do we want to inform others of our abilities and potential contacts which might be useful to them? Or, do we want to impress them to assuage our insecurities?

Perhaps you can think of times when you've tried to convince yourself of your own value by seeking affirmation from others. *New York Times* best-selling author Dr. Paul Pearsall approaches it this way:

> *"Try to be a little more alert to your automatic competitive mental default state. Notice how you seem to automatically compete with others for a better life rather than connect with the good life you have right now ...You will be asked to rethink your definition of success. . . . The rewards for your change of mind can be immense."* [6]

Ironically, in my coaching work, I have found that arrogance is actually most prevalent among managers with low self-esteem. It is not, as one might suspect, the most confident managers who are full of bluster and conceit. Rather, it is frequently a case of "Big hat, no cattle." It seems that a lack of confidence drives these managers to overcompensate with all sorts of dysfunctional behaviors. What's more, they are often unaware of their behavior, dismissing feedback about the public's perception of them as misinformed. When I have been able to focus the coaching on the manager's many unique gifts and talents, and how the manager can maximize them to best serve others, the arrogance diminishes quickly.

> *"Why are you unhappy?*
> *Because 99.9% of everything you think,*
> *And everything you do,*
> *Is for your self,*
> *And, there isn't one."*
>
> Wei Wu Wei

Like many other negative coping mechanisms, arrogance is nothing more than an attempt to satisfy one's self-esteem needs—albeit in an unhelpful way. It is both unattractive and alienating, and the minor satisfaction and assurance it affords is usually short-lived (hence the need to frequently repeat the associated behaviors). It is an indication of a life built on a false foundation; a life that continually needs to be externally validated and shored up by a false public image; a life built entirely on an external facade. This is not to say that arrogant managers are not intelligent, capable people. They are, or they would not have made it as far as they have. They just don't *believe* that they are.

As Leader Coaches, we need to not only be aware of what this arrogance signifies in our own lives, but also what it tells us about what is going on with the Talent. The Leader Coach can be an instrument of change for someone who has developed this damaging behavior. By bringing your expectations of greatness to the Talent, and recognizing and validating her natural gifts, you offer her a whole new way of thinking and being. She may simply need to hear: "You are talented. You do not have to behave this way any longer. You have options."

Freeing Others by Controlling Me

Self-control is a coaching virtue. By exercising self-control, we curtail our tendency to behave in a manner inconsistent with our values and beliefs. We restrain ourselves from saying unhelpful things to the Talent. We do not let our own needs get in the way of satisfying the Talent's needs.

Attempting to control others, on the other hand, is completely detrimental to the coaching relationship (and every other kind of relationship). It suppresses creative opportunities, restrains spontaneity and, in doing so, dooms the coaching process. The Leader Coach who is unable to manage his need to control will drive the natural vitality and creativity out of any coaching encounter.

How do we know if we are controlling? For me, there are three warning signs. First, if I am doing any more than twenty-five percent of the talking, I'm usually controlling. It's difficult for me to speak that much without taking control of the conversation. Second, if the coaching session is rich with my own brilliant insights and advice, I am controlling. The session needs to be rich with the Talent's thoughts, not mine. Third, when my sentences begin with phrases like "You should ..." or "You really need to ..." I am definitely controlling. Try it yourself next time you feel yourself becoming a backseat driver in a conversation. Pay attention to what you want to have happen and how, and then *don't* try to make it happen. Watch yourself. Feel yourself squirm, and practice saying nothing.

Self-control requires that you take a backseat and throw the keys to the Talent. "Here, why don't you drive?" You may know you're a good driver, maybe even a better driver, but you're not driving now. Someone else is. You're the passenger and need to enjoy the freedom of watching the Talent do the driving. You're looking down the road together, not knowing where the next turn will take you, but your hands, as Leader Coach, are off the steering wheel. You might suggest directions when asked, or alert the Talent to a danger he cannot see, but you do not take over the wheel. You have the privilege of sharing the journey, but you cannot direct the journey nor can you determine its destination. This is *not* your journey to direct. In fact, when you come to the humbling realization that you have no idea which destination is best for the Talent, you will have achieved the zenith of the coach's role.

Living it First

As a Leader Coach, you must first apply the principle of appreciation to yourself. Self-esteem depends on looking at everything and everyone, including yourself, through the same lens. To truly see another with an appreciative eye, you must be able to look at yourself the same way. It's difficult, if not impossible, to help someone else fill their self-view with positive images when yours is not equally positive. Accept and embrace your own current success. Identify your gifts and talents. Be confident in the value that you bring simply by nature of being you. Focus on your inherent worth. And perhaps most importantly, honor your big mistakes and failures as life's lessons. How do you do this? You decide to. The habit of appreciation is a decision you make and a discipline you keep.

Have your own challenging high performance development plan. Work towards your own aspirations, because when you do this you gain respect and appreciation for yourself. It's only when this self-respect reaches your deepest level that you can bring your whole, authentic self to your conversations with others. When you can do this, you can hand the keys to the Talent, sit back, and enjoy the ride. This journey is not about you—and thankfully, you no longer need it to be.

> *"He who sets a very high value upon himself has the less need to be esteemed by others."*
>
> Samuel Butler

The process of developing our self-esteem also includes recognizing our personal reactions to insecurity. When we look closely, often we find that our insecurities have just been repackaged. We usually respond by second-guessing ourselves or by worrying about what others think. Sometimes we make excuses or extraneous comments, seeking reassurances to relieve the discomfort of listening to that anxious, afraid internal voice. What situations trigger that nagging insecurity for you? How do you react? Can you trace these feelings back to anything specific in the past? It is likely that we will never entirely eliminate insecurities from our lives, but as we learn to identify them and the situations that bring them out, we will become more knowledgeable about their origins. Our self-doubt is then lessened because our awareness enables us to be more conscious and intentional in our response. We can see insecurity for what it is and not allow it to drive us to behave in manipulative ways. We can choose to smile at this very real human fear and take a higher road.

As writers Kouzes and Posner have asserted in their time-tested work, *The Leadership Challenge,* leadership development is, at its core, self-development. We can only know and relate to others as well (or as poorly) as we know and relate to ourselves. Shift the initial focus to yourself. Challenge yourself to gain the necessary self-appreciation to bring that true self—with all its imperfections—into the coaching relationship. When you can do this, you will have earned the credibility, and the demotion, needed to challenge others to perform at their best.

While the principle of self-esteem is simple, its practice is not. One's quest for self-respect and self-appreciation is not something that can ever be finished. It requires constant self-appraisal and assessment. We can gain it or lose it with each decision we make, and so it is forever in flux. Professional coaches are acutely aware of their own reactions to feeling inferior. Experience teaches us that everything in the coaching relationship begins with the coach. First, we must use ourselves as an instrument to model authenticity. By doing so, we enable another to do the same. We cannot run or hide from ourselves and our own work. Jon Kabat-Zinn wrote, "Wherever you go, there you are."[7] The good news is that it is always within our power to make our next decision one which contributes to feeling proud and better about ourselves. There's always another chance!

❋ TRY THIS

Be intentional about making your next few decisions and make only decisions that you know will make you feel proud. They don't have to be big choices: do you need that second latte of the day? Can you wait an extra twenty seconds to hold the door for the person behind you? Note how easy it is to feel good about yourself and how quickly this occurs. Consider what new decision habits would raise your self-esteem.

When we feel good about ourselves, we tend to make better choices. Hence that well known truism—success breeds success. In the same way, failure creates more failure: we make a poor decision, we feel bad, and because we feel bad we make another poor decision. And so the cycle continues. This simple truth is useful to remember when leading ourselves and others: make others feel good about themselves and they perform better. Make others feel badly about themselves and they perform poorly. In the words of Henry Kissinger, "A reputation for success tends to be self-fulfilling. Equally, failure feeds on itself."[8]

In her book, *Confidence: How Winning Streaks and Losing Streaks Begin and End,* Rosabeth Moss Kanter says that regardless of what kind of team you're part of, good feelings tend to breed success, and success breeds further good feelings which leads to greater success and on it goes.[9] To coach effectively, those good feelings need to start with you.

Becoming a Leader Coach is not about being perfect. It's about being fully you.

How can you tell if someone has high self esteem? Above all, she is comfortable in her own skin. She is not boastful because she doesn't need to be. She is clear on who she is and, because she is working towards her own highest goals and dreams, she does not feel threatened by the successes and life-paths of others. In fact, a person with high self-esteem is also curious about other paths that are very different from her own. She is inspired by the success of others, rejoices in it, and uses the good feeling it generates to propel herself further along her own path. A person with high self-esteem is aware of her flaws and shortcomings, is willing to look at her situation from various perspectives, and is able to be honest about what she finds. She has a good feeling about her own value, which makes her able to recognize, acknowledge, and employ her unique gifts and talents readily in the service of the Talent.

The great Leader Coach does not feel the need to bring his own insecurities to bear on his relationships with others. He is aware of them, but has the strength *not* to act on them at the expense of others. He does not permit these insecurities to direct his behavior. He has a positive feeling about himself and, because of this, he is able to focus his attention on others and relate to them with honesty, understanding, and truth, without needing to make the conversation about him and his own limitations and challenges.

> *"With a healthy sense of self, we feel at ease ... we're centered within a state of contentment. We're not too hard on ourselves; at the same time, we're wise to our own little tricks. We know how we get slippery. We know when we're trying to get away with something. We're comfortable looking at ourselves honestly."*
>
> Sakong Mipham

When you reach a place where you value and appreciate yourself, the people around you instinctively know and respond to you more positively. People with high self-esteem are easy to be around. They don't judge themselves harshly, and because of this, we do not feel judged by them. In fact, we feel that we are accepted by them just the way we are and we seek them out. At the same time, they set a high bar for us and in their presence we want to live up to it.

What does all this have to do with creating significantly higher performance within your organization? Simply this: in the presence of a Leader Coach with high self-esteem, people perform better. They are motivated to take risks and approach challenges with a positive attitude. When people feel valued, they bring a better authentic version of themselves to their work, and by so doing, they inspire others to do the same. It creates the ripple effect of self-esteem, fostering a community of more content, secure, and productive people. These are people who have the confidence to say "I don't know" or "I made a mistake."

Remember that quiet voice in your head, trying to be heard over the booming voice of insecurity? The one which reminds you of how skilled you are, how much you have achieved, how much you have learned, and how much you have to offer to others? When you turn up the volume on that little voice and see yourself in the very best light, you will have the internal resources to put yourself aside, focus fully on another, and earn the credibility you need to become a coach.

❈ TRY THIS

Ask yourself:

What are the small but important things you know you need to do daily to feel at your very best?

When did you feel most alive, most like you? Reflect upon a time when you thought to yourself, "This is what life should feel like!" Think about what it was about those times that made you feel so alive. What made those moments so personally fulfilling? How can these moments become a habit?

What are the thoughts you think most frequently? Which thoughts are useful for you or others? Which ones are not?

Think of a person who you just like being around. What is it about that person that makes you feel so good about yourself in their presence? Practice being that person for others.

We treat others as we treat ourselves. When we are judgmental and hard on others it is often because we are judgmental and hard on ourselves. Reflect on how you have treated others this past week. It may tell you how you have been treating yourself.

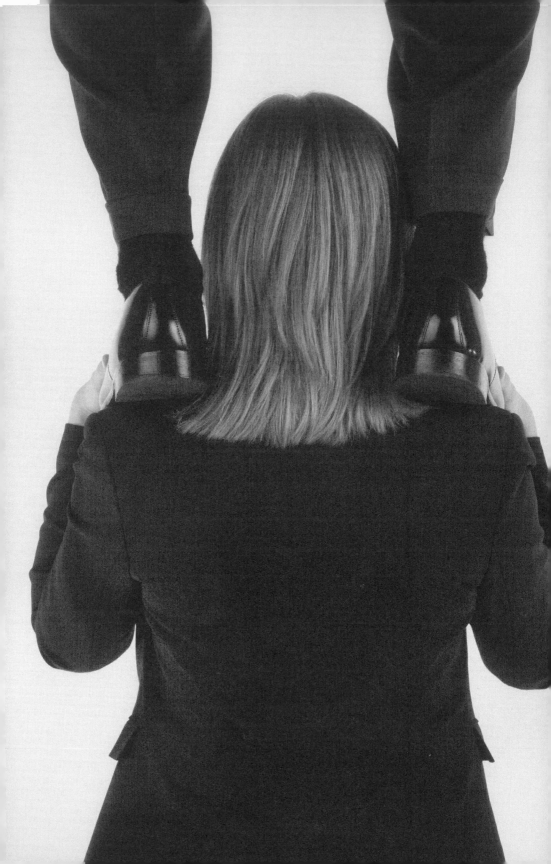

6

Noble Intention

Noble: Lofty or illustrious in character, worth, or dignity; magnanimous, high-minded, morally elevated; of high rank, of ancient or illustrious lineage; belonging to the nobility; magnificent, grand, stately, splendid, imposing; excellent, fine, admirable; valuable, pure (of metals). ...

Arthur L. Hayward and John J. Sparkes,
The Concise English Dictionary

Why do you coach? What's your intention behind it? Is it to correct performance problems, to help others be more like you, or to be seen as someone who is smart and experienced? Do you want to feel useful, helpful, or feel like the boss? Certainly, none of these are malicious intentions, but they all need to be managed. Yes, even the motivation of "just wanting to be helpful" needs to be kept in check.

How can this be?

I often ask workshop participants the question, "When is the help you give unhelpful?" After some reflection, they generally respond, "When I make the help about me and my need to feel useful rather than focusing on meeting the Talent's needs." Despite having the best of intentions, we all do it. We want to be so helpful that we make it about us and our needs and, in so doing, fail to truly help others.

> *"The best answers to many of our most perplexing problems are often already tucked away in the far recesses of our own heads! We sometimes have trouble getting to them, and then, typically, we go around asking others for help. Very often what we are looking for (even if we cannot express it in so many words) is not advice, but help in thinking the problem through for ourselves. Advice-giving, in fact, often undercuts this process."*

Jut Meininger

51

Central to the thesis of *Unleashed!* is that gifted and talented people already exist within our organizations, but that many of them are not maximizing their potential. Talent is everywhere! It's waiting to be unleashed! And the unleashing process is the primary role of the Leader Coach.

When you, as Leader Coach, recognize how much you have to offer others, you can turn that empowering knowledge into a tool to guide others to similar self discovery. To enter into the coaching relationship, it's crucial that you have high self-esteem. It's only through quiet confidence in your own abilities that you can approach another with "Noble Intention."

And what exactly do I mean by noble intention? Simply that in the moment where coaching takes place, you are completely dedicated to the development of the Talent. You suspend your own needs and issues, and focus exclusively on the advancement of the other person.

It's easy to *say* that you need to have noble intention when you coach others, but in *practice* it requires a great deal of effort. You must be aware of your own skills and talents, as well as your shortcomings and defeats, and then be able to put those things to the side in the coaching moment. Above all, you must act with intention. It is not by chance that the effective Leader Coach dedicates selfless attention to others.

How Much Help?

If we truly have noble intention, we bring all our resources into the coaching relationship. This may include time, knowledge, experience, even connections. What does it take for you to approach the Talent with hands open and full? Do you ever hold back that timely insight, that resource, that opportunity? Who will know? What harm will it do? What if it's just a small thing? At a recent wedding ceremony, I heard a marriage celebrant say, "We're always told not to sweat the small stuff, but it's the little foxes that spoil the vineyards in a marriage or in any relationship." In a coaching relationship, too, the small stuff is critical. It is these seemingly inconsequential points that contribute to making Great Expectations coaching so effective; it may be the small gesture you think no one noticed that they remember you for the most.

It's possible to have a coaching conversation *devoid of* noble intention without the Talent ever knowing. But you will know. Once you start down the coaching road, you become an expert on yourself; you become very aware of your true intentions, whatever they may be, and you will no longer be able hide from yourself. You know immediately when you have held something back and denied the Talent your best coaching.

Remember back to the discussion of self-esteem? Once you start to think like a coach, each time you don't coach in complete accordance with your great expectations for yourself, you chip away at your own self-worth. Not only that, but that nagging voice you were earlier telling to "shut up" will have more ammunition. It won't be silenced until you do what you know is right for the Talent.

If you're thinking this is hard work, you're right. Noble intentions don't just materialize. The process involves taking deliberate, considered steps to ensure that the interests of the Talent are of primary concern at all times. A Leader Coach who has noble intentions has made a conscious decision about how she will approach the Talent. She has made the choice to see the Talent with appreciative eyes in order to unleash his potential, even if it means temporarily sacrificing her own needs. This is a Leader Coach who is truly committed to seeing the Talent perform at his very best.

Noble intention is both a mental and emotional discipline. We put on the attitude of noble intention like we put on clothes each day. Think about the Talent and adopt a stance of noble intention toward him in your mind. If your mission in life is to see his top performance unleashed, you will automatically prepare yourself before your next encounter. You will take a proactive role, rather than leaving the meeting of two minds to chance. As Leader Coach, you make a conscious decision to orient your whole self towards another person in the coaching moment. The development of the Talent is now your mission. It is a high calling indeed.

How will the Talent know that you have noble intentions toward him? What will it look like from his side? He will look forward to his time with you. He will see you as someone who believes in him, someone who sees his unrealized potential. He will see you as a person of stature who looks beyond the here and now, who wants others to see their own exciting new possibilities. When he meets with you, he will sense that you are there for him. He will feel well respected and well regarded by you, no matter what. He will appreciate your thoughtful questions and the way you listen with intent and engage his responses. He will feel comfortable sharing his dreams and fears and his gains and losses with you. In effect, he will grant you the right to be his Leader Coach.

Interestingly, the Talent will also be a little afraid of a good coach because you will frequently make him uncomfortable. There may be times when he dislikes you because you voice challenging ideas and perspectives. However, he will know deep down if you have truly acted with noble intentions; some part of him will hear the message, perhaps only recognizing the truth at a later time.

When I look back on my own career, I can see now that my best coaches did not merely view me as a person to be transformed for the betterment of the organization or a problem to be fixed. Rather, they were people motivated by the opportunity to facilitate my own transformation. They found meaning and reward within the coaching relationship. They became excited about seeing me reach my own potential—a level of success they knew was possible even when I failed to see it myself. Having recognized and accepted their own abilities, these men and women were able to put aside their needs in order to focus everything they had on my development. In those coaching moments, they offered all their gifts and talents to serve me. Because they did so, their impact on my career and my life will never be forgotten.

I will say it again. As a Leader Coach, you are the instrument. To find the best in an individual, you must first find the best in yourself. To inspire others, you must first discover your own sources of inspiration. Nurture your passions and you will find the way to nurture the passions of others.

I hear many leaders ask, "How do I motivate my people?" The answer is simple yet perhaps jarring—you don't. Motivate yourself and others see you as someone with passion and excitement, someone they want to impress, someone they want to follow and emulate. Your motivation blazes the path for theirs.

The people who are reverently remembered after they die are usually the ones who gave selflessly to others and contributed to something greater than themselves. Often these people set out to help one person at a time, without regard for their own fame or fortune. Fame and fortune may follow, but that was not their original intention. Mother Teresa did not set out to be famous. She set out to do what she knew was a most noble task—serve the poor and the outcast. She was passionate and fearless about her work and gained respect wherever she went. We don't usually think of her as a marketplace icon, but she became an effective, globally influential humanitarian leader simply because she acted on what she knew was good and right, day in and day out. This was a woman who lived all aspects of her life with noble intentions. She once wrote about a CEO whose whole company exuded the same:

> *"Once I went with the head of a big company to his factory in Bombay, where over 3,000 people were working. He had started a scheme among them where they all gave something to feed the people in Asha Dan, our home. I had gone there to thank them and to my surprise I found that many of his employees were disabled. I was also*

struck that he knew nearly all of the workers by name and as we went through the factory, he had some greeting or word to say to everyone. ..." [10]

There is no doubt that Mother Teresa lived an authentic life with noble intention. The Leader Coach can walk in the footsteps of people like her every day by choosing a mindset that says "I genuinely care about this person's success." The Leader Coach who travels through the organization this way will be distinctive, will enjoy high self-esteem, and will be known by her actions. She will leave a legacy.

Who Owns the Agenda?

In the coaching conversation, the Leader Coach is entirely focused on the Talent (her abilities, her challenges, and her dreams). As coaches, the more we remove ourselves from the agenda and pass it over to the Talent, the greater the impact the coaching relationship will have. This means putting our own wants and needs to the side and allowing the conversation to be completely directed by the needs and ambitions of the Talent.

COACHING IMPACT

Can you suspend your own needs for a time? Can you genuinely care enough about another person to help him perform at his best? Can you choose to love him when you might not like him? If you can, you have the foundation to be a great coach.

✤ TRY THIS

Today, have one conversation in which you focus solely on another person. Focus the entire conversation on that person's agenda, making it valuable only to her. Put your needs and wants aside in this one conversation. Notice the results.

It has been said that in communicating with others we are usually trying to do one of three things: hurt, help or impress. Watch yourself today. Notice when you choose to speak, and get curious about the intention behind your words. At the end of the day reflect back on your most frequent intentions.

In every conversation, there is always a high road we can take. Notice today when you take this road and when you do not.

How High Can You Coach?

Here are some questions you may not have considered before: Can you coach someone to a higher level of performance than you have achieved yourself? Or, does some small part of you feel threatened by the accomplishments and success of others? Do you unintentionally subject others to your own limitations? How high can you really coach?

I readily coach others to succeed when it's clear they are working on performance issues that I have mastered. However, to coach for performance beyond my own achievements, I need to exercise discipline. I must work hard to ensure that my focus remains on the Talent's potential and that I do not sabotage his efforts by projecting my own fears and self-imposed limitations onto him.

I often hear organization leaders attribute much of their success to hiring people who are smarter than they are. This may be true, but I see little evidence of these same leaders encouraging their "smarter" employees to *perform* higher than they do. I believe that most of us are naturally inclined to coach others up to our own level of performance and not beyond. It's not that we consciously keep others down but rather that we have that all-too-human tendency to see ourselves as the model of good performance. And I'll admit it, I'm no different. When I look out at all the challenges facing our organization, a not-so-little voice inside me says, "Why can't they all just be more like me? That would fix our problems." But what if instead I asked myself, "Why can't they be more like themselves?" That really would create a higher performing, higher achieving organization! To see this level of greatness in others and to coach others towards it requires the noblest of intentions.

Usually—thankfully—we do not intentionally stunt the development of the Talent. But intentionally or not, it happens and its impact is enormous. This behavior looks different for everyone and, chances are, you're the only one who will really know when it's happening. However, there are some common cues that may help you identify this subtle form of sabotage.

In your coaching conversations, do you ever hear yourself saying any of the following?

"Starting a new business is risky, you know."

"You need to protect the career you have built."

"I would encourage you to be realistic about this."

It is human nature to project not only our own beliefs about what's possible but also our own fears about the risks involved in performing at a higher level onto other people. As a Leader Coach, you need to ask yourself: "Am I prepared for the Talent to succeed beyond anything I have imagined or thought possible?" If you can answer with a resounding "yes!" then you are likely approaching your role as Leader Coach with noble intentions. And you likely know the answer to the question: Why do I coach?

❊ TRY THIS

Look back on your career and tally up the number of individuals who have grown past you *primarily because of your influence.* If you run out of fingers, be proud of yourself. If you come up short, now's a good time to challenge yourself to coach with noble intentions. Now is the time to ask yourself, "Why do I coach?"

Part 3

A PERFECT PARTNERSHIP

> *"Some day after we have mastered the winds, the waves, the tides and gravity we shall harness the energies of love. Then, for the second time in the history of the world, man will have discovered fire."*
>
> Pierre Teilhard De Chardin

Imagine that tomorrow somebody new comes into your life. This is a different kind of person who looks right past your smiling personality, your typical defenses, the insecurities you've worked so hard to mask, and the failings you're ashamed to admit, let alone accept. This person seems to see only you. Imagine this new person in your life sees all of you and accepts you for who you really are—the individual who wants to be special, who desires to contribute at the highest levels and make a difference in the organization. At the same time, this new person also sees how your personality, defenses, and insecurities get in the way of you performing at your best. He knows when you subtly sell yourself short in your work and career, in pursuing your passions and dreams, and in your expectations for the future. And he won't let you get away with it any more.

Because this person sees the real you and cares, he will not accept anything less than you are capable of becoming. With a deep appreciation for who you are, this person confronts you with a degree of honesty that does not allow you to deny the truth of your potential. At the same time, he recognizes clearly that this is *your* challenge—not his. The only thing that's certain is that this new person will not be satisfied until you are doing your best work.

What would it be like to have just such a person so completely on your side?

Now, imagine what it would be like to *be* that person for someone else.

When the Leader Coach is able to appreciate the best in the Talent; confront her with her own talent, aspirations, and potential; and hold her accountable to perform at her best, the result is a relationship that is nothing short of a *perfect partnership.*

7

Appreciation

"Let us treat men and women well; treat them as if they were real. Perhaps they are."

Ralph Waldo Emerson

A few years ago, I belonged to a group of representatives from oil and gas companies based in Calgary, Alberta. We met occasionally and brought in keynote speakers to address subjects of particular interest. I'm sure that you have heard more speakers than you care to remember, so you know the drill—once she's finished, a representative from the group gives the speaker a gift, thanks her for her time, and everyone applauds. In our group, we did things a little differently. We made a point of giving our speakers a gift and a hearty round of applause as we introduced them, *before* they spoke. It was our way of getting ourselves into a non-judgmental mindset by thanking them in advance for a presentation we already knew was going to be excellent. As a group and as individuals, we had already decided that it was going to be great and that we were going to get something from it. We entered our experience with what I now call *appreciative expectation.*

What if you were the kind of person who believes that the success of others is just as important as your own? How would that change the way you live your life? I know that in my life, the times when I have excelled the most have been the times I have been in the presence of people who believed that their success was dependent upon my success. These were people who believed in me and valued my contribution. They saw gifts, strengths, and talents in me that I *wanted* to see in myself but couldn't, and they challenged me to take risks that scared me. They asked me to put my talents to work when I wasn't even sure that they even existed in the first place. They saw something special in me and I trusted them enough to look for it in myself. These people all gave me the gift of appreciation, the gift of truly seeing talent and potential, focusing on it, and helping me unleash it.

An appreciative relationship is one in which you see the very best in the Talent, *expect* the best from her, and guide her towards seeing and expecting the same in herself. The Talent emerges from the coaching relationship with new self-knowledge and newly discovered great expectations for herself and her abilities.

The power of a positive, appreciative relationship is not a recently discovered principle of human behavior. Socrates and Plato both believed that all individuals possessed inherent wisdom and talents, and could make significant contributions to humanity by developing these. In modern Western thought, the idea can be traced back to the 1950s, most notably in the work of psychologist Carl Rogers. Rogers believed strongly that a climate of trust and respect was essential to facilitating a person's ability to develop in a positive and constructive manner and created a therapy model around this theory.

Initially, Rogers called this process "non-directive" therapy, highlighting his belief that the client, rather than the therapist, should take a leadership role in the relationship. He later changed his description of the process to "client-centered" therapy, noting that while the therapist may take the backseat in the relationship, the client nonetheless looked to the therapist for guidance. Even if the therapist tried not to direct the session, the client would still seek and find some degree of guidance. He described his sessions as "supportive, not constructive,"[11] and likened the experience to learning to ride a bicycle. When you teach a child to ride a bike, you cannot just tell him how, nor can you hold him up the whole time. He has to try it out for himself and fall down a few times along the way in order to learn.

Rogers believed that the client should be responsible for determining what needed to be changed, coming up with his own suggestions for improvement, and ultimately deciding when the therapy has been successful. Thus, while acknowledging the role of the therapist in the relationship, the primary responsibility for the direction of therapy lies with the client. "If I can provide a certain type of relationship," Rogers explains, "the other person will discover within him/herself the capacity to use that relationship for growth and change, and personal development will occur."[12]

Roger's theory garnered much attention among psychologists and therapists in the 1950s and 1960s and remains influential today. But his ideas are also applicable outside of traditional counseling relationships and are invaluable to the practice of high performance coaching in the workplace. We human beings prefer to work with people we like, and who like us. We may say (and even believe!) that we don't need to be friends with our colleagues in order to get the job done but none of us really wants to go to work in the morning feeling like no one is on our side. We seek out people who genuinely like us and actively avoid those we think don't like us or who are cold, unapproachable, negative, or inconsistent. Why are dogs "man's best friend"? Because they are always happy to see us. They appreciate us and love us even on our bad days. They see past our negative qualities and seem to focus on only the very best within us. And, we love them for it. Such is the gift of appreciation.

Appreciation cannot be faked. You either truly believe in the potential of another human being or you do not; either way, they know how you feel.

A Shift in Thinking

In 1987, David Cooperrider and Suresh Srivastva published a groundbreaking paper entitled "Appreciative Inquiry in Organizational Life."[13] In it, they outlined what they called the Appreciative Inquiry (AI) method for organizational change and development. Essentially, AI takes Rogers' ideas about client-centered therapy and applies them to organizations instead of individuals. As its name suggests, AI aimed to identify, support, and perpetuate the very best in an organization through structured questioning. Cooperrider and his colleagues recognized the motivation people gain from their own success and suggested that pointing out and celebrating success in an organization, rather than focusing on its flaws and failures, results in greater improvement in overall performance. Furthermore, they argued that when suggestions for change are based on the experiences of people within the organization—things they are already doing in some way—people will be better able to relate to them and therefore be more willing to change.

According to Cooperrider and Srivastva, "organizations change in the direction in which they inquire."[14] An organization which looks for problems to fix will find and focus on problems; one that seeks the positive things within it will succeed in identifying more and more of what is already working well and focus on doing more of those things.

AI is the difference between believing that "organizing is a problem to be solved" and believing that "organizing is a miracle to be embraced."[15] It succeeds by multiplying the good behavior it focuses on, while putting aside the poor performance it no longer wants. The same principle is used in training racecar drivers: look at the wall and hit the wall; look at the road ahead and make the turn skillfully. Like racecar drivers, organizations go in the direction in which they focus their attention. It's not about changing people, but about inviting people to be a part of an organization that is going in the right direction.

Winston Churchill's appeal to the beleaguered British people in the darkest days of the Second World War is an excellent example of how focusing on the abilities, skills, and resources of the individuals within a group can foster a positive attitude and inspire the group as a whole to persevere. Even in the most difficult of times, we can find signs of life and hope if we look for them. The things we choose to pay attention to and the attitude we have towards change and development can make all the difference to the results we get.

A few years ago I was considering going back to school, and I was really anxious about the application process. I knew what I wanted to study and I knew which school offered the best program, but I was sure that I was reaching way beyond my limits to even apply there. So I applied to several other institutions just hoping that I would get into *one* of them. I remember talking about it with a colleague and telling her in hushed tones where I had wanted to apply and why I hadn't. She completely dismissed the idea that I wouldn't get in and eventually talked me into filling out the application. I remember thinking, "Well, if she thinks I can do it, I might as well try—one of us is bound to be wrong." She proceeded to spend the next six months operating under the assumption that I had been accepted, though I had yet to hear back from the school. At first, I was horrified. What if people heard her talking about it? I didn't want anyone to know! People would think that I was completely full of myself! And it would be even worse when I was rejected, as I was sure I would be. It seemed to me to be completely presumptuous to even apply, let alone go the extra step of believing I would be admitted. But my co-worker's confidence was infectious, and gradually I started to see myself, and my potential, through her eyes. By the time I got the letter in the mail, neither one of us was surprised that I had in fact been accepted.

As Leader Coaches, our goal is to assist the Talent in moving beyond a negative view of his abilities in order to heighten his awareness of his own value, strength, and performance potential. In so doing, we assist the

Talent in overcoming the limits he has imposed upon himself, and the possibilities available to him become enormous. We are charged with the task of seeing the Talent at his absolute best, appreciating who he *really* is, and inquiring into his performance from that perspective. When we bring this attitude into the coaching relationship and we are unwavering in our perspective, the Talent begins to see himself in this same light. Great coaching leaves a legacy of personal power. As a result, the Talent gains a fresh sense of control and influence over his own future, his career (*what* he does), and his performance (*how* he does it). He begins to take the best possible version of himself as the starting point for all his self-reflection and planning, and starts to see his own remarkable possibilities. One of my coaching colleagues is fond of saying: "I love it when my clients really seize the opportunity to become the CEO of their own careers and I become irrelevant." For me, that says it all.

8

Confrontation

"So absolutely good is truth, truth never hurts the teller."

Robert Browning

Consider for a moment the number of family members, friends, and co-workers with whom you interact on a daily basis. How many of them do you believe tell you this absolute truth described by Browning? Probably not many.

Now consider the reverse. How many of these individuals get Browning's level of truth from you? Most likely, the number is embarrassingly small. Why don't we tell this truth if we know that it is in everyone's best interests and, as Browning suggests, doesn't even leave a bruise?

Hearing the truth is a rare thing indeed. As a leadership development coach and consultant, I'm in the business of personal change. In my own life, however, I actually quite dislike change. It's much easier to ask my clients to change than for me to do so myself. I would just as soon go on with life the way it is right now, thank you very much! I'm also not particularly easy to approach with either criticism or praise. I've honed my skills at trivializing and deflecting this information, and I'm also quite prepared to belittle the messenger if he becomes too persistent. In these interactions, I've always found it easier to give than receive. A fellow coach summed up my approach this way: "Feedback is great as long as you don't get any on yourself." But on the too-infrequent occasions when I actually listen to what is being said, there's something quite exhilarating about the result. As a coach, after all, my first job is to work on myself.

Think about this question: What important topic in your own life have you been avoiding that you wished someone cared enough to broach with you? Take a moment to digest the full implications of this question. Sit with it. Write it down and read it over a couple times. Really let it sink in.

What was your first reaction to this question? How did it make you feel? Anxious and afraid or excited and liberated? It's the kind of question that stares at us blankly, expectantly, demanding a truthful answer. Do you find its raw honesty intriguing? The question confronts us at a deep level, as such questions do, challenging us to give an answer that we probably already know but are not quite willing to acknowledge. Answering it honestly requires us to change something in our lives: possibly our habits; probably our attitudes; and, in the most extreme case, our beliefs. The reason I deflect the criticism and praise is not because I believe it to be untrue, but because I'm afraid it just might be true. And if it is true, I have to make some changes! And, in the case of the praise, I have to live up to a higher standard!

The Leader Coach is not a dispassionate judge who enumerates the Talent's countless flaws, nor is she a sightless cheerleader blindly dispensing plaudits. While Great Expectations coaching takes a distinctively appreciative line of inquiry and seeks to identify the best in others, it's not warm and fuzzy coddling. In fact, effective coaching requires us to challenge others with excruciating honesty and candor.

"Truth, like beauty, is when unadorned, adorned the most."

Unknown

Courageous Encounters

The Leader Coach is a master of confrontation, but not in the traditional sense of the word. The word "confrontation" is usually defined as a conflict between people's beliefs and opinions. I prefer to define it as a courageous encounter with the truth—whatever that truth might be.

The role of the Leader Coach is to confront the Talent's ideas, perspectives, and assumptions, and in so doing, enable him to find possible new ways of acting and thinking. To the great coach, confrontation means holding up a mirror so that the Talent can come face-to-face with his perspective on his current situation, abilities, aspirations, and potential, and move beyond the limits he has set for himself.

The word *confrontation* usually evokes the notion of providing negative feedback or the feeling that we are going to be challenged by or faced with an enumeration of all the things we fear we are doing wrong. But what if confrontation was a positive action? Consider what it would be like to confront someone with his own natural talents and potential. Confrontation is equally about challenging the Talent with the good stuff. In fact, rather than focusing on his weaknesses, great coaches spend more time confronting the Talent with his own potential and then challenging him to live up to that potential.

Telling the truth is a perilous endeavor. We tend to do so only when the degree to which we care for another exceeds the risk and discomfort in doing so. We risk confrontation when we care deeply about another person and when we genuinely want to see them thrive. This is the paradoxical gift of confrontation. We confront others when we love them enough to not *not* speak the absolute truth. Some people call this "telling the truth in love." Great coaches care enough about the Talent to suffer the pain of this quality of truth-telling.

So how often do you tell others the truth, the *real* truth—what you are really thinking, feeling, and wanting and what you see in them? Give this a moment of serious consideration. Reflect on your key relationships and as you think of each, consider how honest you have been in that relationship recently. How truthfully have you communicated your thoughts—negative or positive—to the people in your network? We often equate the words "tell the truth" with our tendency to withhold negative information or feedback. Sadly, there is an overwhelming tendency to withhold positive truths as well.

Most of us believe that we're truthful. During leadership development workshops, I often ask participants to rate themselves on their personal level of honesty within their organization. I ask them to declare how frequently they tell the complete truth. By far, the most popular response is "almost always." It's interesting, however, that when I poll others in their organization about how frequently they are told the complete truth by their leaders, I most often hear a response of "sometimes." Why the gap?

We may avoid telling the complete truth more often than we're aware. It's not that we are intentionally dishonest (though recent history has certainly been rife with enormous integrity breakdowns in senior corporate management), but rather, that we are trained and conditioned to communicate what we believe to be appropriate in the circumstances. Over time, this business-speak pervades our communication processes and significantly impairs our ability to be seen as consistently honest. In fact, evidence suggests that tempering the truth is a behavior learned from an early age and can become largely automatic. As children, we were told to think before we spoke, and when we didn't, we quickly learned the consequences. If we weren't careful with our words, we could anger our parents, embarrass ourselves, lose friends, and incur the wrath of teachers. Therefore, as adults we are accustomed to analyzing our thoughts before we share them and holding back the pieces which we decide are not appropriate. We carefully manage our communication with others, sparing both parties the anxiety and discomfort which so often accompany unwelcome or uncomfortable truths.

Striving to be considerate of another's feelings is one way we show our respect and demonstrate that our intentions are noble. Consider for a moment that our desire to *not* hurt others may actually be the most hurtful thing we can do. When our words are anything less than completely truthful, our coaching effectiveness is impaired. It is only when our best intentions are paired with *unusually truthful* communication that high level coaching occurs.

The Power of Truth

Truth is a powerful tool. It is the fuel of high performance coaching. It can free someone from disillusionment and allow her to set a new course. It can expose an unrecognized lie, or it can jolt us out of mediocrity and into a whole new way of living that we might never have imagined or dreamed of. Truth can open new reservoirs of untapped potential. And when the Leader Coach curbs the truth, coaching stalls.

When I catch myself withholding the truth from a conversation, my instinct is to justify this behavior by telling myself that I am really doing it for the other person's own good. Upon reflection, however, I find that my real motivation is an uncomfortable blend of both arrogance and fear. My arrogance is in play when I believe that the Talent is so fragile that he can't handle hearing something I believe to be true. But am I really so powerful? Is he really that breakable? If I am not wallowing in my own power, I'm usually simply afraid. My fear comes to the forefront when I convince myself that sharing the truth will produce some kind of emotional outburst from the Talent, making him unnecessarily uncomfortable. In reality, I am protecting myself from the discomfort of intense emotional involvement.

What opportunities for growth is the Talent missing if we lack the courage to speak? What if we are the only person to ever dare offer honest words to someone who truly needs to hear them? Coaching is too important to dance around doling out vague hints about what is really on our minds.

Imagine you were the Talent and your Leader Coach wanted to tell you her honest (and probably accurate) perspective on a situation that concerns you? If you later learned that she held back, what would you think of her? Would you think she was being helpful or unhelpful? What would you prefer she do?

Great Expectations coaching requires you, as Leader Coach, to associate truth with love and confrontation with kindness. Truth is inextricably tied to noble intentions. When we realize that truth is related to caring about someone holistically, we can appreciate the privilege and importance of being the bearer of such truth to the Talent. Telling an affirming truth is as important as telling an admonishing truth, and a great Leader Coach is committed to both.

Great Expectations coaching is about removing the obstacles which lie in the way of each person achieving the greatness within him. Confrontation and courageous encounters with truth are parts of this process. Recently, a woman shared with me how her boss had remarked that a certain guest speaker would never be invited back again. Apparently the speaker had talked too long and ignored the time allocated to him. She said to her boss, "But he will never know the reason why he isn't invited here again. Maybe he will continue to make this mistake everywhere he goes. What if you were the only person who ever decided to tell him the truth?" How often do we miss an opportunity to remove a hindrance to higher performance because of reluctance to confront?

Often, when we interact with someone regularly either socially or at work, we develop a certain instinct, or intuitive knowledge, about them. You might call this a hunch. As often as not, these hunches are correct, but how often do we act on or express them? My instincts might tell me that my friend is drinking too heavily. Will I say anything to him? Will I express concern or even blurt out what I'm thinking? What would happen if I did? Risky business, isn't it? Perhaps a colleague has been complaining for some time of not feeling well and my instincts tell me she needs to immediately check that out with a physician. Something is wrong. Am I simply a fear-monger or am I expressing real and instinctive concern for her wellbeing?

In his popular work *Blink,* Malcolm Gladwell sheds light on this ability to know something without making a conscious effort to do so. His research suggests that when assessing a situation, the brain works on two levels—conscious and unconscious. At the unconscious level, we can reach a conclusion in seconds, without even knowing we have done so. The brain sends signals through sweat glands, for example, long before we consciously come to the conclusion that something is amiss. Gladwell uses the example of a handful of art historians who experienced this phenomenon when confronted with a marble statue purported to date from the sixth century B.C They instinctively knew it was a fake, even though scholars and scientists had laboriously worked at a conscious level to wrongly conclude it was genuine. Gladwell's book supports the notion that we can act on that impulse, that certain intuition, with a high degree of accuracy.[16]

More often than not, we prefer to push these rapid conclusions aside rather than take a chance and ask a dumb question. We procrastinate and take our unspoken thoughts home.

Why do we not ask more "dumb" questions? We seem to make the assumption that if we do, others will think less of us (or more likely, that we will think less of ourselves). If we are the only ones asking questions like this, everyone else must be much smarter than us. We don't want to lose face, be ashamed, or seen as ignorant by our peers, so we wear a mask of perfect comprehension, pretending to understand. And yet, as a coach I have learned that we need to welcome, not fear, a response to a well-meant comment or question, even if it is negative. Our words tell the Talent that we care enough to risk looking foolish and having to deal with an uncomfortable response. If we didn't care, we wouldn't invite the possibility of embarrassment.

Recognizing and Risking the Truth

Part of the difficulty in telling the truth is that most of us are not fully aware of what it is we are feeling in the moment, and even if we were we would be hard pressed to articulate it. This is why after a particularly taxing conversation, we spend time replaying it over in our mind, trying to decipher exactly what happened and then often wishing we had said or done something differently. Even when we do notice how we feel in the moment, we are often afraid to voice it for fear of hurting another, or we avoid it because we don't want to feel uncomfortable. Rather than take a risk we choose to say nothing, or communicate a watered-down version of what we are really thinking. Often we blatantly disregard our truest thoughts, much to the detriment of everyone involved in the conversation.

"To believe your own thoughts, to believe that what is true for you in your private heart is true for all men—that is genius. Speak your latent conviction, and it shall be the universal sense; for the inmost in due time becomes the outmost—and our first thought is rendered back to us by the trumpets of the Last Judgment ... A man should learn to detect and watch that gleam of light which flashes across his mind from within, more than the luster of the firmament of bards and sages. Yet he dismisses without notice his thought, because it is his. In every work of genius we recognize our own rejected thoughts: they come back to us with a certain alienated majesty. Great works of art have no more affecting lesson for us than this. They teach us to abide by our spontaneous impression with good-humored inflexibility the most when the whole cry of voices is on the other side. Else, tomorrow a stranger will say with masterly good sense precisely what we have thought and felt all the time, and we shall be forced to take with shame our own opinion from another."

Ralph Waldo Emerson

If only recognizing the truth were easy! Then we would all speak it more. However, telling the truth requires that we advance our conversation from the level of politeness (where the unspoken contract is "don't push me and I won't push you") to a higher level of honesty ("I care about you enough to risk saying this because I feel you will ultimately benefit from hearing it").

Confrontation is difficult because it requires three fundamental considerations. In order to confront someone, we must first be able to recognize our own thoughts and feelings in a situation. We then need to trust that our feelings contain valid information worthy of sharing. And finally, we must assess whether sharing our real thoughts and perspectives is worth the risk.

And once we know *what* we have to say and *that* we have to say it, the question becomes *how* we can say it best.

When I look at the people who have most positively impacted my life, I find that many of them had that unique blend of courage and love that enabled them to tell me things that others would not—things I *needed* to hear. They confronted me because they cared about me. It is my experience that most of us have had at least one person in our lives who has done this for us and has been remembered and cherished for it. Great Expectations coaching is about being the person who cares enough to confront others with such truth.

Ironically, for many of us it is as difficult, if not more so, to be confronted by our own greatness as it is to face our faults. You cannot un-ring a bell. Once confronted by our gifts and talents, we can no longer deny the magnitude of our potential. Suddenly, there exists an unspoken obligation to rise to the occasion. A tension has been created between what *is* and what *is possible.* However, many of us actually collude with others to *not* be confronted. We establish a relationship based on pseudo-mutuality; the unspoken contract that says "I won't expect more from you if you don't expect more from me."

> *"Truthfulness. He will never willingly tolerate an untruth, but will hate it as much as he loves truth... And is there anything more closely connected with wisdom than truth?"*
>
> Plato

The conversation we need to have is often the instinctual conversation. We don't need to search for the "best" or "most appropriate" response and we don't need to worry about getting it right—it's our perspective, uncensored and uncut, which is needed. As much anxiety as there can be behind its telling and receiving, when confronted with the truth, people generally feel honored and special. Though we often deny the truth when just in our thoughts, it's remarkably easy to recognize once it has been given voice. This doesn't mean we always want to hear it, of course, but for the most part, we have respect for the fact that someone had the courage to voice it.

Why then, when we offer people what we consider to be the truth, is it so often rebuffed or not heard? Is it that people are that defensive or closed off? Perhaps it's our delivery; our truth, though valid, is said in conjunction with another truth we don't intend, or with less-than-noble intentions.

Help or Harm?

The feedback we give as Coaches is about more than just the words we use. Often, it isn't the things we say but the *way* we say them that communicates our main messages and really makes an impact. Our words are like lyrics in a melody. You can love the song, but violently disagree with the words. Of course, you can also dislike the song, but appreciate the lyrics. And just as we listen to music mostly for the melody, when we give feedback as coaches what comes through most clearly to the Talent is the way we speak. What he is really listening for and responding to is our truest intention, the answer to his question, "Are you trying to harm me or help me?"

A child once wrote in an elementary school test that the Golden Rule says, "Do unto others before they do one to you." We sometimes forget to treat others the way we would like to be treated, or more to the point, how *they* would like to be treated. When engaging in confrontation as a Leader Coach, it's helpful to think empathetically. As the saying goes, "People don't care how much you know until they know how much you care."

It's important to come away from the coaching conversation knowing that you've said what you wanted to say in a way that others hear and understand. When the Talent leaves, will he be enlightened and challenged, or disillusioned and angry? The goal of the Leader Coach is for the Talent to depart the session feeling inflated, regardless of the content of the conversation you have just had with him. When you confront the Talent, whether it is regarding his potential or lack of performance, your job is to provide him with a perspective he cannot get anywhere else. He will probably remember your words and how the conversation made him feel for a long time. Simply put, when you confront with understanding and intention sourced in honesty and kindness, the Talent will respect and trust you, and your coaching will have a remarkable effect.

The Shortest Distance Between Two Points

Hearing the truth is not always easy for the Talent. As a result, the coaching conversation can quickly become uncomfortable. Think back to a time when someone said something to you that really put you over the edge and made you absolutely furious. You probably stomped out of a room, left a party early, or slammed a door. But was there some truth in what was said? Upon reflection, were you over-reacting because you did not want to be confronted with the issue? I have personally had coaching clients become so angry they have terminated the meeting, essentially kicking me out of the office or stomping out of the room, only to return after a few minutes of reflection. As coaches, we need to learn to not take the Talent's anger personally, to persevere with our message to him, and to stick out these moments of discomfort.

When a conversation becomes uncomfortable, our most common reaction is to keep our truest thoughts and feelings to ourselves.

Interestingly, we often feel perfectly comfortable having the conversation we should have had with the Talent with someone else instead. We use the third person as a conversational surrogate so that we do not have to endure the anxiety which comes with sharing difficult (and therefore dangerous) truth with the person to whom it should be directed. Behavioral psychologists call this process triangulation. To the rest of us it is simply known as gossiping, complaining, and blaming.

When we anticipate that a conversation will be uncomfortable, it is natural to want to avoid it—and the other person! The Leader Coach recognizes this, knows that the conversation needs to happen anyway, and goes straight to the person in question.

❃ TRY THIS

Decide that you will no longer triangulate. From now on, speak directly to the concerned party—and to no one else—about what is really on your mind. No more water-cooler talk. No more "he said, she said." In both your professional and personal life, become the kind of person who does not talk about others in their absence, unless it is to honor them and their work.

Just One Conversation

When we have a conversation with someone, we should be having only one conversation in that moment; a conversation in which what we are saying and what we are thinking are in perfect alignment. It does not mean that we simply speak the truth as we think it. Being able to confront others requires more from us than simply blurting out our thoughts, which can come across as choppy and reactive. By the same token, it demands more than *holding back* our real thoughts simply because we're afraid of the impact they might have. Engaging in coach-like confrontation means mastering the art of saying what needs to be said and doing it in a way in which the truth of it comes through.

Even if we doubt the value or relevance of our internal conversation, we still need to find a way to share it effectively with the Talent. If we do not, a part of us will be disengaged and unable to focus fully on the spoken conversation. Sharing our internal conversation is a way of keeping ourselves engaged in the interaction. Even if what you put out there does not ring true for the Talent, speaking up has two important effects: it keeps you fully present in the conversation, and it gives the Talent something to react to.

It is not the role of the coach to determine the value of the information we give. The coach's job is to put it out there, with noble intention, for the Talent to use or not use as she sees fit.

Pay attention to your next several conversations, whether with friends, family, or those in your professional life. Is the conversation you are having out loud the same as the one going on in your head? Notice if and when the conversation separates. What truths do you know that you are withholding from the external conversation? When we conduct two conversations simultaneously, something is going on that needs our attention. As Leader Coaches, our goal is to pay attention to that second conversation, not in retrospect, but in the moment the conversation takes place. It takes practice and focus, but the voice in your head contains important truths that need first to be acknowledged, and then addressed in the coaching conversation.

People instinctively know where there is a disparity between their external and internal conversations. Something doesn't feel right. There is an underlying dissonance between what we are thinking and what we are saying, and we no longer feel free to express ourselves. Often we want to have the internal conversation but don't know how to bridge the gap between the truth we know in our heads and the surface-level external conversation. We feel a distinct tension between these simultaneous conversations, and we respond by putting an invisible barrier between the other person and ourselves. It's as if we quietly slide a screen across our hearts, but not so quietly that the other person doesn't know. They do know. Our smiles and reassurances don't ring true. They sense our withdrawal from the conversation and are aware that we have become less forthcoming and straightforward with our observations. They know we are holding something back.

"You're Better Than This"

As a young man, I loved to play hockey. I think there is something about the unrefined intensity of the sport that brought out my primal emotions and provided a temporary refuge from the modern world. Maybe I just liked being a warrior for a moment. During one particular hockey game, a coach for the other team said something to me that still rings in my ears. This was an especially rough game and I was deep into my primeval behavior (read: I was playing dirty). Late in the game as I was skating past the opposition bench, I saw the coach leaning forward to give me a verbal blast. Hockey coaches are renowned for their ability to deliver a searing, expletive-laced communiqué in a matter of seconds so I didn't think too much of it as I approached him. But this man's words were unexpected and haunt me to this day: "Hey you, number seventeen," he shouted. "I've been watching you. You're better than this!" I was pierced to the core. He may as well have kicked my skates out from under me. At some level I already knew that my behavior and level of performance were beneath me, and he had confronted me with what I already knew to be true. To this day, whenever I find myself opting for the lower road, his words ring crystal clear in my head … *"You're better than this!"*—the confrontation of the true coach.

A Lighter Touch?

After a particularly difficult coaching session that was probably more emotionally-charged than it needed to be, my client, leaning in for full effect, asked, "You are a bit of an in-your-face coach; are you this way with all of your clients?" This gave me pause. Does confronting the Talent mean we need to be "in his face" all of the time? I suggest not. Mariners know that most sailing requires the lightest of touches. Anything more causes the boat to swerve and lose momentum. Many times, the Leader Coach needs to use a light touch to help the Talent navigate through the waters of change. The Talent will rarely know how hard we are actually working to give him the freedom necessary for their great expectations to be realized!

Using a lighter touch means paying attention to what you want to do or say and asking yourself whether your words will be an improvement on silence. Does it need to be said? Does what you want to do need to be done? Or, would the Talent be best served if you did nothing? Sometimes doing nothing is the most difficult and profound thing we can do to assist another.

Do It Anyway

Even after many years of coaching senior executives, it's still not easy for me to confront people with the truth. Over time, however, I have learned to recognize when my internal voice is telling me something that I need to share. And as I mentioned earlier, I do not particularly enjoy being confronted either. But if someone comes to me and says, "Gregg, this is difficult for me to tell you, but I think you need to know this," I find that I am open to the message and grateful to the messenger. Why? Because the messenger clearly has my interests at heart and cares enough about me to suffer some discomfort on my behalf. Most of us don't recognize our first moment of true confrontation because it doesn't feel the way we expect it to. In much the same way that courage is really about being terrified of something and doing it anyway, confrontation means being afraid of what your knowledge might mean for the Talent and telling her anyway, believing that no matter where the conversation leads, there will be good at the end of it.

❄ TRY THIS

Reflect back on the question posed at the beginning of this chapter: What important topic in your own life have you been avoiding that you wished someone cared enough to broach with you? Thinking about your answer, what would someone need to say or do to get your attention regarding this issue? How could a coach best confront you so that you would finally take action on it? How might you use this approach when confronting others?

9

Accountability

"Each person has inside a basic decency and goodness. If he listens to it and acts on it, he is giving a great deal of what it is the world needs most. It is not complicated but it takes courage. It takes courage for a person to listen to his own goodness and act on it."

Pablo Casals

One of my professors at graduate school had an annoying habit of asking me a particularly vexing question whenever I complained about the dreadful behavior of others in my life. No matter what I was complaining about, he always replied, "What's your part in this issue?" I still remember how that question irritated me. To a young man so sure that he was in the right and so sure that he was on top of his own game, his question was quite insulting. He just didn't get it. It was like he didn't understand how wonderfully satisfying it was to blame others for my troubles. Couldn't he see how much I loved the role of innocent victim where I did not have to fuss with the nuisance of personal responsibility? Why couldn't he just let me wallow in my blissful state of self-righteous indignation? He couldn't because he was a true coach who held me responsible for my own behavior and my own life; a coach who knew that personal accountability and personal development are two sides of the same coin.

"People are always blaming their circumstances for what they are. I don't believe in circumstances. The people who get on in the world are the people who get up and look for the circumstances they want, and if they can't find them, make them."

George Bernard Shaw

Nix The Sounding Board

When I hear coaches being referred to as "sounding boards," alarm bells go off. This usually means that the Talent wants the coach to act as a scratching post for their chronic complaints—about their boss, staff, customers, co-workers … the list can (and does) go on and on. Some would suggest that the Leader Coach needs to "create a safe space" for the Talent to vent and clear her issues. I disagree. The more venting (read: whining) the Talent does, the deeper she falls into the illusion of being the victim of circumstances, rather than the architect of her own future. The deeper she etches this sense of helplessness onto her self image, the more difficult it becomes for her to take personal responsibility for her own performance and the other aspects of her life which she has the power to change herself.

The Authority To Act

Accountability is most frequently thought of in terms of results and consequences. We typically define accountability by using words such as responsibility, answerability, and liability. I prefer to enlarge that definition by incorporating the concept of *authority to act.* This is a subtle, yet important distinction. It means that with the responsibility for results comes the power to take whatever actions are necessary to bring about those results. When the Talent truly believes that he is accountable *and* has the power to act, the coaching process becomes fully empowered.

> *"I think one must finally take one's life in one's arms."*
>
> Arthur Miller

❊ TRY THIS

Think about something that you have complained about recently. It could be a work related issue, a health issue, or even a personal relationship issue. Ask yourself, "Have I done absolutely everything to achieve the outcome desired? Have I taken full accountability for what needs to be done to improve the situation?" When I ask this question of myself, my answer is usually, "No, I have not."

Think of an issue that is important to you and particularly troublesome in your work life right now involving someone who is performing below par. Ponder for a moment on the fact that, if this person changed the way he performed, this issue would be improved substantially. Now put that thought away.

Construct a wall in your mind that will not allow you to access this perspective. For a time, completely ignore his responsibility for the issue. Now ask yourself "What's my part in this?" Once you have answered this question as honestly and thoroughly as you can, go to this person and share your findings, taking great care not to raise the issue of the other person's responsibility. Note the results. Repeat as necessary.

Accountability and the Coach

The Leader Coach has two key roles regarding accountability: one is to model accountability in his own life; the other is to expect accountability from others.

> *"More often than not, all a complaint is is an unfulfilled request. A need we haven't met or a question we haven't asked."*
>
> Rhonda Britten

As a coach, you are continuously on display, and those you coach will know whether or not you take full responsibility for your own performance. Coaches have an obligation to demonstrate a high level of accountability in their own lives if they are to expect the same from the Talent. Great coaches have an air of responsibility about them. When something goes wrong, they don't blame others; rather, they examine their own choices and accept responsibility for their part in the results. I don't mean that they think that everything comes down to them—great coaches are the opposite of self-centered. They are, however, fully and actively responsible for their own part in the outcome of any situation. They focus their time and energy on their part in the relationship—the piece that they control—knowing that they always have control over how they choose to respond to external events.

In The Puddle

Skilled coaches have clarity regarding the boundaries of their accountability: they are acutely aware of that line that separates their responsibilities from those of the Talent. They know which issues they own and which are owned by the Talent. They know which part of the conversation they are responsible for and which part belongs to the Talent. As seductive as it may be to do otherwise, the true coach is ever vigilant not to cross that line.

When the Talent is wrestling with a very difficult issue, it is extremely tempting to dive in and help her solve *her* problem. The great Leader Coach knows that it is the Talent's responsibility to solve these problems. But this can be oh-so-difficult when you are oh-so-sure that you have the solution and you oh-so-badly want to be helpful. I have seen many clients struggle with a problem so intensely and vociferously that they cannot find their way out. I call this being "in the puddle." It is analogous to sitting in the middle of a puddle, splashing and shouting that you are drowning in an ocean. It is very enticing for the coach to reach down and pull the person out of the puddle. The great Leader Coach resists this urge and challenges the Talent to stop splashing, take an honest look at his situation, stand up, and walk out of the puddle. By leaving the Talent "in the puddle" until he is ready to act, the Leader Coach demonstrates a commitment to personal accountability.

Changing the Conversation

Can the Leader Coach force the Talent to accept personal responsibility for her performance? Of course not. As one of my college professors was fond of saying, "Each of us is accountable for being accountable." We can, however, have a great deal of influence on the Talent through the choices we make regarding our part of the conversation. The recipe is straightforward: when we assume the Talent is fully responsible for his own behavior and future, and remain strictly in Leader Coach role throughout the conversation, the Talent is compelled to either assume personal responsibility or allow the conversation to dissolve. It is through the power of the coaching conversation that the Talent is pressed towards accountability.

How does this work in an actual conversation? First, it is important to understand some theories about how individuals interact when they converse. When a person participates in a conversation, she is compelled to define herself by the role she takes on. Think about all the different roles we assume in conversations: helper, teacher, playmate, adversary, complainer, counselor—to name a few. The role we choose determines much of our behavior in the conversation. For example, when we assume the role of Leader Coach we are defining ourselves as one who is concerned with self-development, reality, adaptation, and personal responsibility. When we choose this role, the Talent must choose a congruent role, one which can interact with the Leader Coach's area of concern, or the conversation ends. It is through this dynamic that the Talent is encouraged to assume personal accountability.

Psychotherapist Eric Berne developed a model of conversation he called transactional analysis. Transactional analysis provides useful ways of studying coaching conversations and the part they play in encouraging personal accountability. Berne suggested that each person chooses to interact with others from one of three patterns of thoughts and feelings he called ego states; Parent, Adult or Child:

 The *Parent* ego state has two predominant aspects: it is controlling and nurturing.

 The *Adult* ego state, which has no relation to age, is oriented toward pragmatism, adaptation, and autonomy.

 The *Child* ego state is comprised of generally unregulated emotions and feelings.

Berne further suggests that each of us has all three ego states and the ability to move between them in our conversations with others. None is considered universally superior to the others in all situations; however, the Adult is the autonomous mediator of the other states because it is in this role that the individual assumes responsibility for herself and her future.[17]

As illustrated in the following diagrams, conversations that are congruent (or parallel) can continue indefinitely.

Incongruous (or crossed) conversations are unsustainable and need to become congruous or end.

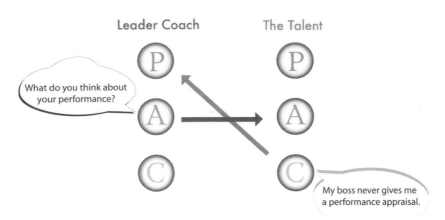

True coaching occurs when both the Leader Coach and the Talent operate in their Adult states, with each taking responsibility for his own performance. It is all too tempting for the Talent to slip into the Child state (either rebel or victim) and the Leader Coach to slip into the corresponding Parent state (director or rescuer), but the Leader Coach must remain in his Adult state and insist that the Talent move up into his as well in order for coaching to be successful.

I am not suggesting that either the Parent or the Child is an inherently negative way of being. When we are in our Child, we can be playful, free spirited, and adventurous. Our Parent, on the other hand, is the piece of us that takes responsibility for a situation, steps up to make things happen, and is central to good leadership. However, there is no place for either of these states in the coaching conversation.

So what can the Leader Coach do to help the Talent move toward accountability? Simply this—when the Talent is not taking personal responsibility for his own performance and future, he will always speak from his Child. If the Leader Coach complies and speaks from his Parent, the Talent can stay in his Child for the duration of the conversation. Here is the secret: ignore the Talent's Child and speak directly to his Adult even if he initially refuses to communicate from this state. By doing this, you create dissonance and a conversation that is unsustainable. The resulting anxiety requires the Talent to either move into his Adult state or terminate the conversation.

If you have raised children, you will recognize this as a natural parenting process used to encourage children to assume more personal responsibility. Parents do this in various degrees of intensity by addressing children as young adults (assuming responsibility) as opposed to immature children (assuming irresponsibility). We ask our children to take responsibility for the role they play in any given situation; our challenge, as coaches, is to continually ask, "What is your part in the issue?" and to hold the Talent accountable for his actions.

Part 4

DANGEROUS CONVERSATIONS

> *"For corporations doing business anywhere, it will be imperative to recognize that truth in communication is going to be regarded as the line in the sand. Workers and consumers alike are going to insist on truth. They will react against communications designed to convince, manipulate, guide or maneuver."*
>
> Ann Coombs

How many conversations do you have during an average day? And how many of these simply function as social lubricants helping you slide through the day without having to address the important issues facing you? How many of them really matter?

Most on-the-job conversations involve the exchange of information, instructions, advice, and opinions and have relatively predictable outcomes. While these conversations are quite suitable for normal business transactions, they are quite ineffectual in the coaching process. Coaching conversations need to be much more potent. They are characterized by purposefulness, emotion, and awkwardness. The Great Expectations model of high performance coaching rests on a unique conversation which challenges the Leader Coach to engage in an intense form of dialogue. This is the *Dangerous Conversation*.

Why "Dangerous"?

A dangerous conversation is akin to a crucible; everything superfluous that is contained in a social conversation is burned away, leaving the most valuable things behind. The dangerous conversation does not unfold without wrinkles; it confronts the questions that need to be asked and challenges the Talent to answer them honestly.

These conversations have no predictable course or conclusion and are fraught with uncertainty for both parties. Coaching often requires the Talent to confront sensitive issues related to his personal performance and aspirations, and challenges deeply-held beliefs and ingrained practices. As a result, the process produces a variety of emotional responses. Over the course of one conversation, the Talent's feelings may range from exhilaration to despair, confusion to clarity, and anger to tranquility. The Leader Coach needs to be able to remain in the conversation regardless of the emotions exhibited by the Talent. Sometimes performance coaching comes perilously close to therapy or counseling; however, it is important for the Leader Coach to recognize that the future is their province, not the past. This helps keep the conversation coach-like instead of therapy-like.

These are *dangerous conversations* because a Great Expectations coaching session is not a fluffy, feel-good love-in. It is a high stakes interaction in which the Leader Coach and the Talent engage in a daringly candid conversation that can evoke a vast range of feelings. As a Leader Coach, your role in the dangerous conversation is to be honest, authentic, and unattached to a specific outcome. In so doing, you create a conversation in which the Talent is able to generate rich new insights and knowledge. To make this happen, the interaction is necessarily unpredictable, unstable, and dangerous.

> ***Dangerous Synonyms:*** *risky, unsafe, chancy, uncertain, unstable, important, conclusive, consequential, crucial, deciding, decisive, desperate, determinative, hairy, hazardous, high-priority, integral, momentous, perilous, pivotal, precarious, pressing, psychological, serious, significant, strategic, urgent, vital, weighty.*
>
> Microsoft Encarta Reference Library 2005

10

Conversations that Matter

"I am not bound to win but I am bound to be true. I am not bound to succeed but I am bound to live up to what light I have."

Abraham Lincoln

Dangerous conversations can only occur when we do not assume an outcome. They occur when we recognize that we do not have the answers for another, but that we do hold the power to *listen* those answers out of *him*. If we let silence do some of the work, we enable the Talent to hear himself say something that he might not know he already knew. Crucially, the conversation is a one-way street. By entering into it, the Talent has decided to explore personal changes, and the coaching relationship rests on him maintaining that commitment. If he goes back on his commitment, the focus then has to shift to examining what got in the way of him following through on what he said.

Non-Attachment

As an external executive coach, it is relatively easy for me to remain detached from what the Talent decides to focus on and what he does or does not do. My only job is to challenge him to live up to his own highest standards. For example, if those standards require him to spend more time with his family than at the office, I coach him to attend to his most important values. However, as a manager within an organization, your task as Leader Coach is significantly different. By nature of your position, you are attached to the Talent's performance. You need to be. Your results are based on how others perform. If you are reading this book, it is because you want to elicit higher levels of performance from those with whom you work most closely. A big piece of this is learning to remain detached from the outcome of the coaching conversation, even if it has a negative impact on your role in the organization.

How do you remain detached when you are, by definition, attached? One way is to recognize that your job as a leader is to bring out the very best that each person has to offer. In order to do this, you need to know what the Talent values most, what he cares about, dreams about, what he is working towards at this time.

Woven through this information you will find the answer to the ultimate coaching question: why does the Talent's performance sit at its current level? Is it because he is comfortable? Is he afraid that he doesn't have better options? Or is it because he is committed to success within this role, but is unsure of the steps he needs to take to excel, contribute, and advance his career? If it is the former, you want to know this now, so that you can coach him to leave his comfort zones and pursue his real dreams. If it's the latter, the sooner you can assist him in identifying his path, the sooner he will be bringing his best game to the organization.

When we engage in a Dangerous Conversation, we are providing the Talent with the time to think about, organize, and articulate his thoughts—thoughts he might have had running in his mind but found himself unable to reconcile for years. Through the listening process, we challenge the Talent to dive deeper into his best thinking, help him to focus, and then, deduce his own best answers.

Walk Away Empty

Have you said everything that needed to be said? Great coaches walk away from a conversation feeling empty. Stepping into the role of Leader Coach is about saying everything you need to say to the Talent so that when you leave the conversation there is nothing left. The conversation is complete. There are no words unspoken and no regrets. It sounds straightforward enough, but as with so many things, the practice is more difficult than the theory.

The goal of every interaction or exchange is to have no regrets, to know that everything that needed to be addressed was said in the moment. We know immediately when we have done this because we feel great. Even if we have a very difficult message for another about his performance, we can take comfort knowing that our work is done. We said everything that needed to be said and we leave with a sense of peace.

Conversely, we also know immediately when we haven't given everything to the conversation. We walk away feeling unsettled, running the conversation and the thoughts we censored over and over again in our mind. Sometimes we even seek out a third party with whom to have a second conversation because we didn't have the courage to be completely candid in the coaching moment. And sometimes—almost as if to add salt to the wound—we later hear another person voice what we lacked the courage to say.

❋ TRY THIS

After your next few significant conversations, notice how you feel.

Do you feel complete?

Did you say everything you needed to say with that person at that time?

Do you feel good about the interaction? If so, notice why. If not, again, notice why not.

Is there something else you wish you had said or done?

Do you feel that you held back in the conversation and if so, in what ways and why?

What did you choose not to say, and why? Any regrets?

This is not to say that we can *always* walk away empty. However, we *can* aim to raise our awareness of those instances when we are engaging in two simultaneous conversations and learn how to bring the one going on in our head into the one coming out of our mouth. This can be very scary. Speaking out for the first time, we often believe that we will make the situation much worse than if we remained silent. And if we mess it up, so what? One of the most amazing qualities humans possess is their ability to forgive. There is always a second chance to go back in the conversation—to apologize and try again. When we approach others with truly noble intentions, they know it. They do not expect us to be perfect, only to be authentic.

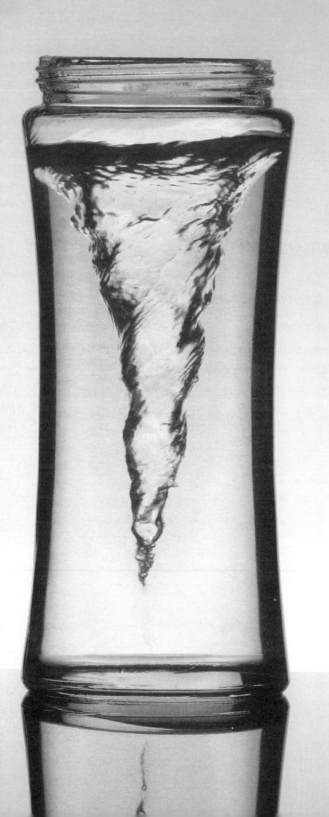

11

The Coaching Flow

*"What matters in the end ... is not the methods but the attitude
behind them. If that is right, the methods work. If the attitude
is wrong, methods are meaningless ..."*

P.W. Martin

Great Coaching Flows

It flows through three phases, namely **Discovery, Creation,** and **Commitment,** which the Leader Coach must navigate as the Talent takes on the often rough and unpredictable waters of personal and professional change. Coaching would be much more straightforward and uncomplicated if one could simply memorize and follow a prescribed series of steps in a pre-established sequence to achieve a specific set of results. Unfortunately, it doesn't work that way. Every coaching relationship follows its own unique course. Think of the coaching process as more improvised than scripted, more spontaneous than structured.

Because these phases are distinct, they are often misinterpreted as a static, linear model for undertaking dangerous conversations. Rather, the coaching flow is, as a client of mine once described it, "an unguided pilgrimage to my best and scariest future." The most effective coaching results are achieved when the conversation is allowed to—and given the space to—move back and forth between the phases as necessary in order to cover territory and incorporate information which is revealed during the coaching process. Thus, the dangerous conversation ends up being more adaptable to the flow of information within each coaching relationship. The following illustration represents the direction of a coaching conversation:

Improvising the Conversation

Phase #1: Discovery

> *"The real voyage of discovery consists not in seeking new landscapes, but in having new eyes."*

Marcel Proust

> *"The significant problems we have cannot be solved at the same level of thinking with which we created them."*

> Albert Einstein

During the Discovery phase, the Leader Coach helps the Talent see his performance and potential through fresh eyes. The Talent is challenged to dig deeper, to ask more of himself than he may have been accustomed to, and to confront a current problem or challenge by gaining a greater understanding of himself through exploration and inquiry.

The first step in the Discovery phase is to help the client understand his current perspective. How does he view his current circumstances? How does he define the challenge or issue he faces? What solutions does he believe are available? Through discovery coaching, we assist the Talent in realizing that his answers come from only one perspective but that by looking at the situation from different angles, a world of new possibilities will open up to him. Together, you can paint a picture of the Talent that gives him a whole new understanding of who he is, where he is, and what he is capable of. Through this process, he will uncover *his own* answers to some exploratory questions, such as:

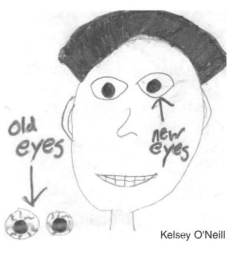

Kelsey O'Neill

- ⇨ What do you most value?

- ⇨ What have been your greatest successes?

- ⇨ Where are you right now? Where do you want to be?

- ⇨ What is most important to you in your job now?

- ⇨ When you are at your very best, what are you doing?

> *"The important thing is not to stop questioning."*

Albert Einstein

When you coach someone through a period of Discovery, your job is to ask some of life's most basic and difficult questions. The Talent does not need to know all the answers right away, but he needs to be curious and willing to find out. The Leader Coach's challenge is also to be curious, seeking the Talent's truth while remaining detached from the response. Discovery is a form of play—caring, unstructured play where the mystery lies within the other person and the outcome is unknown.

Phase #2: Creation

"No great improvements in the lot of mankind are possible until a great change takes place in the fundamental constitution of their modes of thought."

John Stuart Mill

During the Creation phase, the Leader Coach helps the Talent take his new-found perspectives and create possibilities for change. It is about developing, drawing up, deciding on, and generating something new. As a Coach, you challenge the Talent to see opportunities in what he calls problems. It's not about helping him choose between options. People generally don't need help making decisions; they need assistance generating new options and being able to look at those options with a fresh perspective. In coaching, we challenge the Talent to discover other ways of interpreting his situation so that he can see new possibilities and make more effective decisions. The Talent and the Coach use their collective analytical and idea-generating skills to challenge assumptions and beliefs and to look at situations anew.

People tend to become set in a single way of perceiving a situation. This blocks both change and success. Creation coaching is about getting the Talent out of his own way, challenging the self-limiting beliefs he has, and demanding that he operate at an entirely different and higher level. As a Coach, you give the Talent a second pair of eyes where he previously only had one pair; you open up a whole new way of seeing himself and the world.

Phase #3: Commitment

"Do or do not, there is no try."

Yoda

You have used dangerous conversation to help the Talent identify what lies at the core of his current challenge, explore the problem from a range of perspectives, and identify a variety of possible solutions based on his new insights. What now? Your next question to the Talent is simple and obvious: "What do you want to do about it?"

The final phase of the Dangerous Conversation is commitment, wherein the Talent chooses a new perspective and a new way of operating, and commits to enacting the necessary change in his life. This is a much more profound process than simply making a decision to do something new. It doesn't mean saying, "Yes, tomorrow I will make my relationship with our VP of Operations better." Rather, it is about engaging in a personal process of transition in the moment, of recognizing how he owns this situation, and realizing that he needs to change himself—not the other person. Commitment requires that the Talent take a first step towards change right then and there, and that he hold himself accountable for that decision.

When the Talent commits, he brings the conversation to bear on tangible, actionable, realistic next steps. For example, "This week, I will do the following things to improve my relationship with the VP of Operations." These are bite-sized chunks that he can manage and which pertain directly to his own role in the situation. When those changes have been successfully incorporated into his behavior patterns, he then makes a new realistic plan for change. Commitment is fluid, not static; it moves with the Talent as he needs to change.

The greatest challenge of this final and most difficult phase of coaching is for the Talent to recognize that it isn't easy. There are many forces in the world trying to push him back into his previous performance patterns—after all, the way he has been doing things up until now has made him pretty successful. There will inevitably be times when the Talent will be blown completely off course. True commitment is the ability to get back up and keep going, regardless of setbacks. Commitment cannot be rushed into, but once it has been reached, it demonstrates the true power coaching has to deliver sustainable performance improvement.

The path of the coaching conversation through Discovery, Creation, and Commitment is not a linear one. The discussion flows back and forth between these three phases as necessary. There is no defined end-goal, but there is a commitment on the part of both the Talent and the Leader Coach to go wherever the conversation takes them in the development of the Talent.

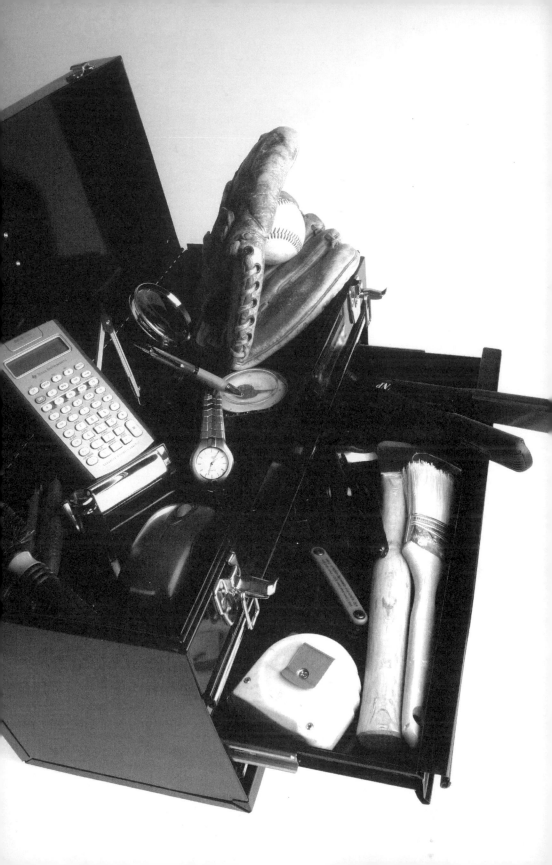

12

The Four Coaching
Power Tools

*"Principles and rules are intended to provide a thinking
man with a frame of reference."*

Karl von Clausewitz

So you've been accepted as a coach, you've entered into a partnership of equals, and you're embarking on dangerous conversation. What now?

Though I firmly believe that it is *who you are,* not *what you do,* that makes a great coach, I also recognize that you will need some tools at your disposal in order to be most effective. In my experience, there are four key tools which are invaluable to coaching work: Acknowledgement, Big Questions, Intuitional Perspectives, and Silence.

Power Tool #1: Acknowledgment

> ***ac·knowl·edg·ment*** *(noun): 1. the act of acknowledging, or the condition of being acknowledged. 2. a sign showing that somebody has seen or heard someone else's greeting or presence. 3. a letter or message indicating receipt. 4. an expression of thanks or appreciation. 5. official or public recognition for services rendered.*

Microsoft Encarta Reference Library 2007

Genuine acknowledgment is a powerful thing. Fully recognizing who someone is and what they bring to a relationship, as well as their personal experiences and challenges, can be profoundly inspiring. There is a traditional Tibetan greeting "tashi deley" meaning, "I honor the greatness in you." Acknowledgment is about honoring and respecting the people you come into contact with. It is, as explained in the Arbinger Institute's book *Leadership and Self Deception,* about experiencing yourself as "a person among people" rather than "a person among objects."[18] Coaching is a difficult road to travel, and as Leader Coaches, we need to acknowledge the Talent for walking down it. Entering into a coaching relationship is a voluntary endeavor, and any individual who consents to do so has the self-awareness to know that he can perform at a higher level and the courage to allow the coach to join this uncertain journey. As coaches, we are well-advised to acknowledge this strength of character early on in the relationship.

> *"Let us treat men and women well; treat them as if they were real. Perhaps they are."*
>
> Ralph Waldo Emerson

A true coach is honest, and that also means acknowledging the Talent's struggles and the mistakes he has made in his self-management and his management of his relationships with others. Nonetheless, we are all, to some extent, guilty of what cognitive scientist Lee D. Ross called the Fundamental Attribution Error—that is, we generally attribute our own behavior to situational influences, but tend to blame the actions of others on character. In my opinion, true acknowledgement of another human being means correcting this fallacy. We know that the Talent has encountered difficulties and made mistakes, but we don't see his behavior as a direct reflection of the kind of person he is. We see his potential in a positive yet honest light, and encourage him to do the same by holding him accountable and insisting that he is capable of better.

Acknowledging is not synonymous with complimenting. Complimenting the Talent can be perceived as superficial or phony, especially when it only scratches at the surface of her true self. Rather than noting your approval of the attributes that are readily apparent on the surface, look beyond personality and social graces to see who the Talent really is, who she has been, and who she is struggling to become. And tell her what you see.

A statement of acknowledgment can take many forms, but it is always explicit about the behavior we want to point out. Something as simple as using the person's first name communicates that you see them and their particular experience. For example:

⇨ "Emily, I have noticed how much work you've been putting into this project and I want you to know that your commitment and dedication have not gone unnoticed."

⇨ "Sarah, I recognize that you have been under a great deal of pressure since you took on this account and think that you've done an amazing job of keeping the team together and delivering quality results."

⇨ "John, I can see you've been really challenged by your project deadlines. How are you doing?"

⇨ "Sam, I can see you have been stretched and challenged by the recent reorganization. I want you to know that I see your persistence in the face of some very difficult challenges."

True acknowledgment is rare and therefore extremely powerful. Most of us lead busy, hectic lives in which we rarely feel heard or seen for who we really are. When somebody pauses and takes a moment to *really* notice us, and to communicate the value they see in us, it can have amazing positive consequences. Often, all we want is to be noticed by another human being. Usually, we don't even want them to do anything beyond simply acknowledging who we are and what we're trying to do with our life. This is just one of the reasons coaching is so effective. In our society, it is all too uncommon to experience genuinely devoted attention; when we do receive it, it can be enough to inspire us to continue to strive for great things.

My friend Keith knows well how powerful a single, seemingly effortless act of acknowledgment can be. In one of his very first jobs, he had the good fortune to work with an extraordinary senior leader named Bill. Everyone in the organization was touched in some way by Bill's authenticity. People felt that Bill acknowledged their importance in the company. Case in point: each year at the company Christmas party, Bill stood at the front door and welcomed each of the four hundred employees who walked through the door by name. "This one act had a huge impact," says Keith. "Imagine being a relatively junior employee walking into the room with your spouse and here is one of the most senior people in the company greeting you by name!" It was more than just a gesture—Bill genuinely cared enough to acknowledge each person and let them know that they were valued. This annual tradition had such an impact on Keith that years later he went back to Bill to ask him how he managed it. Very few people ever knew, but Bill kept a binder with a photograph of each employee, and every year, a week or two before the party, he took it out and studied it, challenging himself to put names to all the faces.

Bill knew the profound effect his acknowledgment had on people, and he put a great deal of effort into making sure it happened. Instinctively, he knew what researchers have shown repeatedly in studies: optimism and pessimism are learned traits. When people work in a positive environment and are acknowledged for their personal value to the organization, they internalize this optimistic assessment of themselves and perform accordingly.

> *"Nothing great was ever accomplished without enthusiasm."*
>
> Ralph Waldo Emerson

The 10 Big Acknowledgments

1. You are a very interesting person.
2. I enjoy working with you.
3. You have a wonderfully distinctive personality.
4. You are obviously a very talented person.
5. I see that you are having a very good/difficult time right now.
6. I think you have great potential.
7. I value your willingness to confront this issue.
8. I see you as quite unique.
9. Your fine work has not gone unnoticed.
10. I like you.

❋ SUSANNE BIRO

My mother owned and operated a local barbershop, and she insisted, like her father had done with her, that I learn the family trade. I didn't want to be a barber, but it was decided I would learn the skill to put myself through school and, in the words of my mother, "have a trade to fall back on."

I spent a total of thirteen years working part time in my mother's shop where she had only one rule for business: Every customer must be greeted as he enters the shop. In fact, this rule was so simple that for a long time I failed to see the complexity behind it. It has only been recently that I have come to realize the incredible business acumen of my mother—a woman who emigrated from Europe in 1966, barely spoke a word of English, and had no formal education beyond the standard eight years required in Europe at that time.

Imagine arriving at her barber shop having just sat in rush hour traffic after a long stressful day. As you open the door you are greeted with a smile by people who are genuinely happy to see you. If you've been to the shop before, you are greeted by name and met with a jovial reception. If this is your first visit, you are acknowledged as a new customer and welcomed accordingly. The day you have just had suddenly disappears, and you find yourself in a friendly place where people are happy you have arrived. The environment is welcoming. You can relax here. You can read the paper as you wait for your favorite barber and engage in the ongoing conversation of the day, or be helped immediately by an equally friendly barber who is available now.

This one act of greeting each customer as he entered the shop kept my mother's business booming! People came back again and again, I believe, because we had created a relationship with every single person. They were no longer just customers. My mother had a way of turning every client into a friend—a friend who came to visit every four to six weeks. These barber visits became a time to reflect on life—the joys and the struggles, the excitement and the challenges. It was a place to laugh and relax—getting a haircut was just an excuse for coming. My mother knew that we were not just in the hair business; we were in the business of acknowledging people. What we offered was time for a man to be recognized as a person rather than as one of his many roles. From the moment he entered the shop, it didn't matter if he was a doctor or a janitor, a teacher or a researcher, a stay at home dad or lonely bachelor. He was seen as Jack, Soli, or Martin and greeted as though he was Norm entering Cheers. He was seen and heard.

I now believe that greeting each customer by name accomplished two complex things. First, it created an immediate relationship with our clients. It said to them, "We see you and we're glad you're here." As a result of this, many clients waited, sometimes over an hour, to get their hair cut. It also created a sense of community. Second, much to their surprise, the habit of noticing and acknowledging others became infectious, and clients found *themselves* greeting others as they entered the shop. There would be days when it was standing room only and still everyone waited happily, warmly greeting and making room for the new person entering. My mother's shop had a rich sense of community which people didn't want to leave; I think some were actually sorry when it was their turn to get their hair cut!

Power Tool #2: Big Questions

"Tell me, what is it you plan to do with your one wild and precious life?"

Unknown

A well-posed question is a powerful thing. Short, simple, open-ended, and challenging, the "Big Questions" we ask force the Talent to look for his own answers, answers he already has within himself. By asking a question, you avoid offering direct guidance or trying to solve the Talent's problems for him. Instead, you challenge him to dig deep within and find his own personal truths. Often, this exercise results in the Talent realizing something he didn't know he already knew and making a significant change based on the newly discovered knowledge.

Coaching is based on the assumption that people can ultimately determine their own best answer. Your role as Leader Coach is simply to ask the questions that bring those answers out. There are an infinite number of questions you can ask, and your task is to find the ones which inspire the most productive self-reflection in the Talent at a given moment. Pose the questions that go deep, open up an unexpected perspective, and provoke change. Intuitively, you will know what these questions are; they are usually the most obvious ones and the ones that first come to mind.

Children do this extraordinarily well: Where do babies come from? Why can't I play with that man? Why doesn't Mommy sleep here any more? Where does God live? Have you noticed how we often become uneasy when confronted with the questions of a child? All of a sudden we are not talking about dinosaurs, SpongeBob SquarePants, bedtime rules, table manners, or the dangers of the basement stairs. The child has sparked a different kind of conversation requiring a different kind of thinking and we can't slide by with pat parental responses. They force us to examine our own assumptions, beliefs, and values and to express what we find in words that a child can understand—no easy task!

In coaching, the power is in the question. Great coaches understand that asking a provoking question is far more valuable to the Talent than any amount of advice could ever be. Phrased in the right way, questions can jolt the Talent into recognizing an unacknowledged truth or a new perspective on his situation and expand his understanding of his own potential. Answering tough questions challenges the Talent to identify and live out his most important values, to pursue his aspirations, and seek to become the very best version of himself.

"Life is an unanswered question, but let's still believe in the dignity and importance of the question."

Tennessee Williams

The following are 60 simple yet provocative questions that I have found useful in my own work. This list is not intended to be exhaustive; it is merely a guide from which you can develop your own questions which pertain more specifically to the situations you address.

The 60 Big Coaching Questions

Coaching for Discovery
About You...

1. How would you describe your personality?
2. What matters most to you right now?
3. In which traits and characteristics do you take the most pride?
4. What important thing have you learned about yourself recently?

Your Future...

5. What excites you most about the future of your organization?
6. What future achievements are most important to you?
7. For what do you want to be known?
8. What about the future scares you?

Your Talents...

9. Where have you achieved your greatest successes?
10. When you are at your best, what are you doing?
11. What would happen if you used all of your natural talents?
12. What can you do better than most everyone else?

Your Job...

13. What consumes your attention these days?
14. What parts of your job do you particularly enjoy?
15. What inspires you?

16. Who do you most frequently blame for your problems at work?

Your Performance...

17. Are you currently doing your best work?
18. Where are you currently being well received?
19. What distractions are influencing you now?
20. If your performance does not change, what will likely happen?

Coaching for Creation

Challenges...

21. Which working relationships are affirming and which are degrading?
22. What one thing impedes your performance?
23. In your career going forward, what might be your greatest regrets?
24. What would happen if you really took your foot off the brake?

Possibilities...

25. How can you expand your world of work?
26. What is the most exciting outcome you can imagine?
27. What one personal change will result in the biggest benefit?
28. If you felt powerful and in control, what would be possible?

Perspectives...

29. What's an entirely different way to see your situation?
30. What would improve if you see it through eyes of wonder?
31. How would others describe your performance?
32. How would others describe your potential?

Resources...

33. If you had unlimited resources, what would you do in your job?
34. What additional resources would be the most helpful?
35. How might you use your greatest strengths everyday?
36. How can you get others eager to be involved?

Change...

37. What thoughts and habits no longer serve you well?

38. What new skills will provide the biggest personal payoff?

39. What actions do you need to take but are avoiding?

40. How can you change your job so you do more of the things you love?

Coaching for Commitment

Expectations...

41. What specific outcomes are you expecting?

42. How important are these outcomes to you?

43. What will be different this time?

44. What do you need to do so you do not have regrets?

Commencement...

45. Which difficult conversation needs to happen?

46. What is the most potent first step?

47. What short-term breakthroughs are necessary?

48. How will you maintain momentum?

Investment...

49. What do you need from others?

50. What sacrifices are you prepared to make?

51. What talents will you rely upon the most?

52. How will you provide the extra energy needed to create the change?

Accountability...

53. Do you trust yourself to follow through?

54. What specific commitments have you made?

55. What promises will you make to others?

56. What promises have you made to yourself?

Stewardship...

57. How will you know when you are on the new road?

58. How might you use your personal power to best serve others?

59. What will you do when you encounter unexpected obstacles?

60. How will you ensure the changes are enduring?

"I don't know the answer, and yet I care."

Kenny Moore

Power Tool #3: Intuitional Perspectives

"Men occasionally stumble on the truth, but most of them pick themselves up and hurry off as if nothing ever happened."

Winston Churchill

"What does it matter how one comes by the truth so long as one pounces upon it and lives by it."

Henry Miller

We may confront through questions, but coaching is not only about asking Big Questions. As a Leader Coach, your job is also to share the ideas and thoughts that seem obvious to you. By doing so, you provide the Talent with something to react to and thereby dive deeper into her own best thinking. As Leader Coach, you have an incredible wealth of experience and knowledge which can benefit the Talent and it is valuable to share this. We do this poorly when we give advice or share our war stories—tales that begin with, "It's like the time when I ... " do not serve to increase the Talent's awareness of her own situation. We do this best when we simply put voice to what is on our mind without censoring our true thoughts, with the express purpose of serving the Talent's development.

Intuitional Perspectives are about blurting out the obvious, saying what is really on our mind—and doing this without being attached to whether or not we're right. Your Intuitional Perspectives are valuable to the Talent because they are authentic reflections of your point of view; they are what you are *really* thinking right now. And, more often than not, they contain some key truths. Does it matter if the Intuitional Perspective is incorrect? Nope, not at all. Given with noble intention, your Intuitional Perspective offers the Talent something to react to and against and through this process helps her determine where the truth lies. The Leader Coach's job is to offer the best intuitive input you have available. Its validity will ultimately be determined by the Talent.

After all, we each bring our own unique perspective, rich with knowledge, talent, skill, and experience to every relationship we enter. We would not fully serve the Talent if we withheld any of these precious resources from our conversation. With every question we ask, we offer ourselves to the client as a tool for discovering the answer. Though I discourage you from simply giving advice or sharing war stories, there is no doubt that your experiences can play a critical role in the practice of coaching. If you cannot share what you think and feel as you listen to the Talent speak, you will be unable to guide them through the challenging and uncertain process of answering difficult questions. It's important, however, to remain detached when you tell these stories, to make it clear to the Talent that you are sharing them for her benefit (not your own), and that they represent *a* perspective, not *the* answer.

Sharing your Intuitional Perspective is fundamental to the coaching relationship. You have promised the Talent complete honesty, and your perspective is the most honest information you have access to. It is the information you have without knowing where it comes from, the gut feelings we all too often ignore or fail to trust. Your intuition is always real, even if your interpretation of the feeling isn't always correct. And though it is never going to be the only information available, it remains a valuable tool for the Talent. Remember your personal detachment from the relationship—communicate what you know and feel, then allow the Talent to do what she chooses with the information. Not an easy task, I know, but it is the most powerful and effective way to share information. It places the onus on her to decide what to do with the information she has at hand and to take responsibility for the choices she makes.

"I do not invent my best thoughts; I find them."

Aldous Huxley

"The intellect has little to do on the road to discovery. There comes a leap in consciousness, call it intuition or what you will, and the solution comes to you and you don't know how or why."

Albert Einstein

The 10 Big Intuitional Perspectives

1. I think you are capable of much more.
2. I find that easy/hard to believe.
3. I think you do not realize how talented you are.
4. I believe you are being too easy/hard on yourself.
5. I think you are avoiding the real issue.
6. I see a completely different future for you.
7. It appears that you are having a hard time letting go of this issue.
8. I think you are afraid to try.
9. I believe you give others too much credit/blame.
10. I think you have great courage.

Power Tool #4: Silence

"Silence is the mother of truth."

Benjamin Disraeli

In coaching, silence carries a lot of weight; just as silence between notes allows us to hear music, so too does silence between the Leader Coach and the Talent allow the Talent to hear his own voice (and thoughts) with clarity. In her two remarkable books, *Fierce Conversations* and *Life One Conversation at a Time,* Susan Scott speaks about letting silence do the heavy lifting. As coaches, our greatest effort goes not into asking or answering questions, but into providing space: a structured environment designated specifically for the Talent to identify and analyze his own thoughts. In this safe space, true reflection can take place and previously hidden solutions are discovered.

I firmly believe that great coaching results more from who you are than what you do. However, it is also important to be able to communicate that information to the Talent effectively. Acknowledgement, Big Questions, Intuitional Perspectives and Silence are all powerful tools which allow you to bring important, provocative subjects to light in the coaching conversation and effect development and change in the life of the Talent.

13

The Coaching
Workspace

"The best way out is always through."

Robert Frost

A coaching conversation needs room to move, to play, to experiment, and to learn. As such, the most important task that the Leader Coach needs to attend to when a coaching relationship is initiated is increasing the workspace. Recently, I was out on the town with a couple who teach ballroom dancing part-time. We found ourselves in a crowded R&B club complete with a live band and a dance floor full of swaying couples. Having never seen them dance, I asked if they minded giving me a demonstration. They agreed reluctantly, and I soon understood the reason for their hesitation. As they valiantly struggled to make their way through the throng, it became apparent that they needed more space in which to do their work. They needed the entire floor, every corner. Similarly, coaching has a need for emotional and psychological space.

To coach effectively, we need room for ideas to flow and new discoveries to be made. We need workspace. The coaching workspace is the area of free movement available to the Leader Coach and the Talent. The Leader Coach's role is to constantly push the boundaries of awareness and knowledge in the relationship and, in so doing, expand the coaching workspace. Coaching is not simply about increasing the Talent's awareness and knowledge. Both he and the Leader Coach need to push their limits outwards in order to expand the common ground available to them.

The Coaching Workspace Model

The Coaching Workspace model is based on the Johari window (developed by Joseph Luft and Harry Ingham in the 1950s) which is a visual representation of how individuals interact, share, and receive information.[19] It has been adapted to the coaching relationship to illustrate that the manner in which information is shared between the Talent and the Leader Coach determines the level of coaching which can take place. Above all, the model seeks to communicate three points which are central to the coaching conversation:

1. **Leader Coach Privilege:** There is always information others know about us that we cannot know about ourselves. We all have a blind spot.

2. **The Coaching Workspace:** The coaching relationship is holographic. That is, whatever plays out in the coaching relationship is being played out elsewhere and so, as a Leader Coach, we can address what shows up in the relationship to most immediately assist the Talent.

3. **Talent Privilege:** The purpose of coaching is to assist the Talent in learning more about himself. It is not about us learning more so we can offer advice.

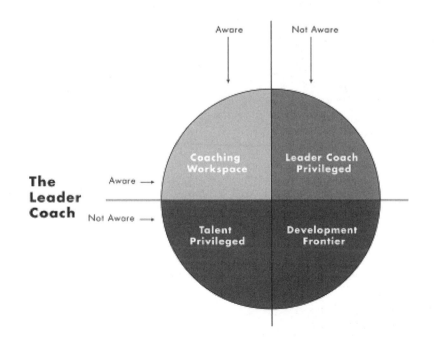

The circle in the Coaching Workspace model represents all the information which exists about the subject on which coaching is taking place. The circle is split vertically, illustrating the division between the information the Talent is aware of and that which he is not. The horizontal division indicates the same separation of awareness for the Leader Coach. The resulting four quadrants are representative of the four different types of information which exist within every coaching relationship: Coaching Workspace, Talent Privileged, Leader Coach Privileged, and Development Frontier.

The size of the quadrants is not static—each can fluctuate, depending on the amount of information given and received by both the Talent *and* the Leader Coach. I have had clients who were unhappy with the idea of being coached and refused to share any information with me. For my part, I was disinclined to contribute many of my insights and feedback because the information I did offer was rebuffed or went unacknowledged. As a result, we had little material on which to base the coaching relationship (see Private, Oblivious Talent below). But I have had many more experiences where the Talent was eager and receptive to the coaching process, shared information openly and listened to and absorbed the insight I offered (see Open, Self-Aware Talent below).

Private, Oblivious Talent   **Open, Self-Aware Talent**

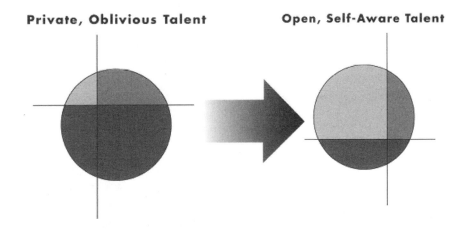

As coaches, it is our job to work with the Talent to push the boundaries of the Coaching Workspace as far out as possible, maximizing the information, and thus the opportunities, available for the coaching conversation.

The Four Types of Information

The Coaching Workspace

The Coaching Workspace contains all the information that is known to both the Talent and the Leader Coach. It includes those things the Talent knows about himself and chooses to share with the Leader Coach, as well as all information the Leader Coach knows about the Talent and shares with him. This includes factual information, as well as emotional and behavioral information—*anything* that the Leader Coach and the Talent know and share with each other about the Talent. For example, the Talent may tell the Leader Coach what particular issue he wants coaching on and how he feels about it. The Leader Coach, meanwhile, may give the Talent feedback on how he might be perceived by others based on his body language and choice of words. When both parties are really listening and receptive to the information being shared, their knowledge base becomes broader and the Coaching Workspace expands.

The size of the Workspace is a direct reflection of how honest, edgy, and powerful the coaching conversation is. When we, as Leader Coaches, ask provocative questions and confront the Talent with a different perspective on their issue, we push the boundary of his awareness outward into his Talent Privileged area, bringing new information into the Coaching Workspace. By the same token, when the Talent believes we have earned the right to coach, he shares information with us about which we were previously unaware. This can include his innermost thoughts, aspirations, and dreams as well as his frustrations, fears, and disappointments.

Talent Privilege

This area represents those pieces of information which the Talent knows, but are not known to the Leader Coach. The Talent will always know more about his challenges and opportunities than you ever can. Imagine, for example, that I am the Talent and you are my Leader Coach. Based on all the information available to you (this book, the Bluepoint website, etc), there is no way for you to know what I, as a child, wanted to be when I grew up. You might guess based on what you know of my career, but you can't know for certain; it is information confined to my Talent Privileged area until I choose to share it. Once I reveal to you that I always wanted to be a Marine Biologist, your boundary of awareness shifts over, the fact becomes part of our common knowledge base, and the Coaching Workspace expands.

If we ask the Talent to disclose something which is privileged, it's important that we are aware of *why* we are asking it. Will it benefit the

Talent, or are we asking it to satisfy our own curiosity and further our own understanding of the situation? New coaches will often try to understand every aspect of the Talent's situation so that they can help solve the problem. But the goal of coaching is specifically and exclusively to assist the *Talent* in learning more about himself and his situation. Surprisingly, the Leader Coach doesn't actually need to know everything about the situation to fulfill her role. It is unrealistic, if not a little arrogant, to think that we could ever understand the Talent's particular challenges as well as he does—as such, there is very little point spending coaching time making sure *we* feel comfortable with all the information available. The questions a Leader Coach asks should have the sole purpose of expanding the Talent's frame of reference on his challenges, opportunities, and personal and professional life. We need to be diligent in asking ourselves, "Is this question providing new insights for the Talent, or is it information he already knows and so it is only being voiced for my benefit?" If it isn't helping the Talent, It shouldn't be asked.

Leader Coach Privilege

No matter how self-aware the Talent is, there will always be information that he will not know about himself. Why? Because we can never experience ourselves as others experience us; there are inevitably things that exist outside of our point of view which we can never see clearly on our own. This is a really important point because many of us have an underlying assumption that we *should* know more about ourselves than everyone else does. If we don't, we think that we're unaware, delusional, or out of touch. Certainly, well developed self-awareness is an important trait, but the fact remains that we can never know everything. This is why, if you ask your closest friends and family to describe you, it is likely that they will all come up with something quite similar—and it is equally likely that their words wouldn't be the ones you would use to describe yourself. Another great example of this is how others tease us by mimicking our mannerisms, and we find ourselves asking, "I don't really do that, do I?" Their answer, of course, is a resounding, "Yes!"

✵ TRY THIS

Ask several of your friends to select three words that best describe you. Very often, your friends will all agree upon the words, and the words they select will surprise you. They will not be quite the words you would have selected for yourself. It is not that you are unaware. It is because others know you in a way you cannot know yourself.

What relevance does this have to coaching? Knowing that some information is not immediately available to the Talent, we can help him receive feedback from others more objectively by recognizing it as coming from alternative perspectives, rather than an absolute truth about who the Talent is. Very often, feedback, especially feedback we perceive as negative, can be difficult to hear because it does not match the image we have of ourselves. We hear it and are disconcerted that others see us in an unfamiliar way, especially because we are well aware of the motivations and intentions which lie behind our behavior. It can be disappointing to learn that we aren't doing enough to communicate our intent, particularly when we have been working hard at it.

Discovering that our truest motivations have been misunderstood can make even the best of us want to give up trying. Understanding that we will always have a blind spot can relieve some of this anxiety and make us more open to and curious about learning the information that lies in the Leader Privilege quadrant. Information in this area can come from instruments such as 360 assessments, as well as from informal conversations with a Leader Coach who cares enough to share it with us. And remember, not all the things one doesn't know about oneself are negative! Much of what a Leader Coach shares with the Talent is about the great skills and abilities which he has yet to recognize in himself.

Gaining insight into how others see us can be a powerful experience. Leader Coaches give this gift to the Talent when they share their perspective with noble intention. We give the Talent information about themselves which he could not otherwise have known, information that he can use in his efforts to develop and achieve his highest level of performance.

Development Frontier

The Development Frontier contains those pieces of information of which neither the Talent nor the Leader Coach are aware. It is the unknown.

Though neither the Talent nor the Leader Coach is aware of it, the information in the Development Frontier certainly exists and it has an impact on the Talent's situation. However, he can only engage with and employ those things he is aware of in his self-development. Just as Talent Privileged and Leader Coach Privileged information can affect, but not contribute to, the conversation until the Workspace is expanded to include it, so too must both the Leader Coach and the Talent become aware of Frontier information before it can become part of the Coaching conversation.

Have you ever learned something about yourself that completely surprised you and everyone else around you? I used to be terrified of public speaking. Twenty-five years ago, I (and everyone else I knew), would have thought the idea that I would make a living as a speaker and facilitator was absolutely crazy. Then in the early 1980s, I took a seminar that really hit home. It was a single comment from the seminar's facilitator which rang true and has stuck with me ever since. During the morning session, I was required to stand up and introduce myself, as was every other participant. And, like every other participant, I was a little nervous. Speaking in front of thirty other professionals was not my idea of a comfortable situation; however, during the morning coffee break, the facilitator came up to me said something that changed the way I saw myself. She said, "Gregg, you have a great speaking voice and strong presence in a room. You should really considering speaking in front of people more often." And then she walked away. I was stunned. For the rest of the seminar, I couldn't get her words out of my mind. "What if she was right?" I thought. What if I was talented at speaking in front of others? My life was changed in that moment. Her single comment opened a whole new world for me. It was a piece of information that existed in my Development Frontier, just sitting waiting for someone to share it with me.

The goal of coaching is to bring as much of the Development Frontier as possible into the Coaching Workspace. However, we can never absorb it completely. There will *always* be information out there of which neither we, nor the Talent, can be aware. The Coach's job is to work with the Talent to actively minimize this space so that high level coaching can take place in the largest Coaching Workspace possible.

Expanding the Workspace

Many limitations are self imposed. We are prisoners of our own minds. We wake up each morning and act out a story we have written about who we are and the role we play in our family, community, and organization. We have a personal narrative about what is possible for us, what can be done and what cannot, and then we live our lives within that script, re-creating and solidifying the story each day. Through the intense and candid dialogue of a coaching relationship, we are able to learn about how we have been crafting these scripts and begin to see where we have placed arbitrary boundaries around ourselves.

One of the greatest values that coaching has to offer is that it demands action. Coaching begins with a conversation, but the real work starts when the Talent goes back to her life and begins to behave differently. Through this process, she learns that previous limitations no longer exist and in fact, they never did. She expands the range in which she can act, and in so doing, increases her 'response-ability.'

14

The Coach's Voice

"Language is power. ... Language can be used as a means of changing reality."

Adrienne Rich

The Power of Language

The artist has the brush, the surgeon has the scalpel, and the conductor has the baton. The coach has words. When he can assemble these words into a special language that challenges and helps others perform at their very best, he will have found the coach's voice, a voice that can be heard above the din of the background noise and idle chatter of our day-to-day lives.

Words can have an incredible influence on others.

"I have a dream."

"We have nothing to fear but fear itself."

"One small step ... "

"Ask not what your country can do for you, but what you can do for your country."

These words inspired people, brought their hearts and minds together to a united cause, and changed the course of history. And though these examples are quotes from leaders who spoke to and motivated entire nations and generations, the power of language is as potent, if not more so, to an audience of one.

❋ TRY THIS

Spend an entire day choosing to use only positive, appreciative language with the people around you. At the end of the day, reflect on the behavior of those with whom you have interacted. Can you identify instances where those words you used dramatically shaped the behavior of others? Enjoy! Repeat as necessary.

Think about the words you use everyday in your working life. You will likely have noticed that the modern business lexicon tends to be quite restricted, confined to words and expressions which are "objective" and from which passion and excitement are conspicuously absent. Business students are taught how important words like *variances, outcomes, assessments, deadlines,* and *professional* are to effective management, but at the same time many MBAs enter the working world, woefully under-equipped with language that truly engages employees and ignites their passion. Managers ask their employees to continuously improve, drive corporate initiatives, and increase margins and then they wonder why their offices are drained of energy and inspiration. And yet what more can we expect when we evoke no emotional responses from employees?

As coaches, the most potent tool we bring to our relationship with the Talent is dynamic language. And just as a carpenter does not turn on an electric saw without knowing how to correctly operate it, we must understand how our words are received and choose them accordingly. Language allows us to connect with people, and our choice of words determines the type of connection which is possible. As leaders and coaches in the workplace, we should strive for honest, visionary, transformative conversations that bring us up against the truth and effect change and development in the lives of the people we touch. The right words can inspire people, ignite their hearts and minds, get them excited about a project, expand their belief in their own potential, and make them want to give more of themselves to their work. And their lives.

Words operate on so many different levels of meaning and implication that we are often not completely aware of the effect they have on our listeners. And yet as coaches, it is our job to be aware. In "Conversations that Matter" (Chapter 10), we discussed the high level of conversation which takes place between the Leader Coach and the Talent. The type of language we use as coaches determines the level that the conversation can reach and how much real progress can be made. Every conversation we have with the Talent is an opportunity, and when we become cognizant of *the way* we say what we say, the impact we make in the coaching moment becomes more intense and more transformative.

One of the greatest strengths of language as a tool for coaching is its flexibility. We can and must mold and shape the words we use so that we're really *saying something* to the Talent. We aren't just parroting the same language back to them, reinforcing their comfortable perspective on the matter. It is imperative that we draw upon our vast toolbox to say it a different way, offer a new perspective, shift the focus of the discussion onto a different target, and incite development and growth in the Talent. There is no list of special coaching words; there is only the knowledge of the function language serves in the coaching process and the careful judgment of the Coach as to what needs to be said, and how.

In its truest form, coaching language is at once provocative and sensitive. It is provocative in that it describes situations in new and sometimes uncomfortable ways, calling our comfortable perspective into question. When I coach, I use very provocative language. I get a sense of the conversation, what is and is not being said, and I start to throw out my ideas. A lot of the time, they go nowhere; the Talent will tell me I'm off course, that my words don't ring true to them, and then the conversation will continue. It's not about my being right in my observations all the time. It's not about me at all. It's about trusting my intuition about what might be missing, taken for granted, or overlooked, and pointing it out. If I'm wrong, I'm wrong. But my job as a coach is to throw the possibilities out there, to use language to unveil new possibilities, and to ask the Talent in that moment to look honestly and openly for truth in them.

Coaching language is also sensitive. When we talk about confronting people with ideas expressed with provocative language, it is easy to begin thinking of the conversation and the language we use in a negative light. But the language of coaching is sensitive in that it ultimately comes from a place of concern and caring for the human heart and self-development. Sometimes my words will get my client's back up or make her extremely defensive, and I usually take that as a sign that we've hit on something important, but the goal is never to stay in confrontation mode. Rather, it is to guide and support her in the process of recognizing and learning from the new, uncomfortable perspective. When this happens, ask the Talent, "Sounds like I just hit a nerve—can you tell me what I did or said that are you reacting to? What has upset you most in what just happened? Are you open to us using this to dive further into Discovery with you?" If she is, you can then ask, "Does this same reaction show up in other relationships? How does that impact your effectiveness?"

When our ultimate concern is for the welfare and development of the Talent, she knows. Human beings are unbelievably good at detecting nuance and intention in the words and manners of others, and if the Talent senses your provocative, challenging language is coming from a place not of criticism but of caring and support, she will allow the conversation to venture into uncomfortable territory.

Above all, the language of the coach is rooted in truth as we know it in the coaching moment. When we speak to the Talent, we give her the truth as we see it, remaining confident that no matter what path that truth leads us down, there will always be good at the end of it. The language of a coach can be edgy and extreme, and include the kind of words which you may never hear spoken in any other context, but which are used in the spirit of developing the Talent. It's not about being right. The language can be symbolic, passionate, challenging, and heartfelt. There is no script in the coaching relationship. There is only one-to-one straight talk in the moment which is completely honest and offered solely for the purpose of developing the Talent. It's about bringing your whole self to the conversation with nothing but your voice as credentials, not holding anything back, and letting honest dialogue develop.

Using your Coach's Voice means finding that special language which resonates with the Talent, which causes him to sit up and really hear what you are saying. In the coaching moment, the Coach's Voice is the catalyst that challenges the status quo, sees possibilities, and demands change. Without using the powerful, quiet, provocative, and sensitive vocabulary of the coach, the conversation will remain perpetually on the surface, and the Talent will never really be forced to register and respond to what is being said. Of course, each of us responds to the complex implications and nuances of the English language in different ways, therefore no one defined set of coaching words works for everyone. Hence the need for you as a Leader Coach to develop and expand your use of the English language—drawing upon concrete business terms as well as abstract and highly personal words. Your challenge as a coach is to unlock the Talent, to engage in high-level listening, to learn who he is, and to discover the particular language which provokes, excites, and inspires him to effect change in his life. The actual words you use will be different for each individual you work with, but for you, the principle of being able to use language in a variety of ways remains the same.

How do you adapt your language so that the Talent can hear you? I like to think of this process as akin to working alongside people from different cultures. When we know that not everyone in the room attaches the same meaning to words and behaviors, we don't take it for granted that our intended meaning will be evident to the person we are speaking with. We know that we need to draw carefully and skillfully on words, examples, and anecdotes in order to communicate effectively. The same is true in a coaching relationship. Our job as coaches is to offer a different perspective, to get the Talent to see something which he had not recognized or acknowledged when looking at himself through his habitual lens. Language is our pivot point, the hinge we can use to turn the Talent's gaze to a different angle, to help him see himself from a different point of view. If we use words that fit in his comfortable perspective, if we don't provoke a response with unanticipated words, we are not coaching.

Using the Coach's Voice is as much about listening as it is about speaking. In your next meeting, notice what you pay attention to and how you pay attention. For example, are you focused on how you are coming across and what others think of you? Or, are you focused on others— what is happening for them and how they are doing? The Leader Coach who can remove the focus of his attention from himself instantly gains access to a huge amount of information about the people around them. When we listen for (rather than to) what is being said, we become aware that in their mundane interactions, people reveal great things about who they are without even knowing it.

Consider this: I recently interviewed a candidate for a prestigious, in-demand position. The candidate had all the credentials and experience that I could have hoped for, and it was clear that she was eager to get the job. Despite all this, I didn't hire her. My decision was based on a single sentence from her interview. It wasn't that she had said something so distasteful that I dismissed her outright, or that her particular mode of delivery was offensive. It was just that in one single sentence, she spoke volumes to me about *how* she thought. I knew in an instant that her worldview was not in line with that of the organization and our clientele. I just knew that this would not be the right fit for her or for my organization. Our words, even if very few, speak volumes about who we are.

Make no mistake, our words *do* reveal us. They tell others what we think about, how we think, and what really matters to us. This is valuable to remember because a large part of your role as a Leader Coach is to notice the language of the Talent. Again, she will most fully reveal herself in what she chooses to focus on and how she chooses to discuss those topics. Everything is information. The Coach's Voice is not just about being deliberate in our use of language. It is also about how we acquire information and what we do with it. When we really listen to other people

we gain information which significantly influences the way we can communicate with them. It shows us their leverage points and guides us in our
search for powerful, provocative language. It gives us the raw material we
need in the coaching process.

I have always liked the idea of artistic unity: that everything an artist
chooses to include in her art is carefully selected. Nothing has been care-
lessly tossed in, nothing is unintended, every piece is necessary to the
creation of the whole. I believe that the art of coaching follows this principle of unity. In the coaching moment, the Leader Coach acts intentionally, every word carefully selected for the service of the Talent. There are no
wasted words, no sentences tossed in to fill empty space, no contributions or observations which are not made with the sole intent of developing the Talent. When a Coach shares a personal experience, its purpose
is to illustrate an important concept for the Talent, and if she feels that she
would only be sharing it for her own benefit, she refrains from weaving
that thread into the tapestry of the conversation.

Think about the experience of meeting someone's family for the first
time. Perhaps you once dated someone who finally deemed you appropriate to introduce to their family (and also finally trusted that you would
no longer judge them negatively once you met their crazy relatives!). Isn't
this kind of a situation fascinating? When you enter into a new family, you
enter into a brand new culture, rich with new and unfamiliar relationships.
Because you are observing from the outside, you are able to see the
human dynamics in a way that those involved in the family cannot. The
moment you walk into a room and meet these new people, you begin
forming judgments. Aside from a few comments your partner may have
made on the way over, your opinion of these people is entirely based on
what they say and the way they say it. You ask yourself questions to
assess and understand the group dynamic: What do they talk about? How
do they talk about it? Who talks to whom? In what ways? Do they speak
well of others, or do they degrade them in their absence? Are they warm
and welcoming in their tone? Ultimately it's their language and the way
they use it which gives you that first critical insight into who these new
people are.

These kinds of social situations don't come along often in our everyday
lives, but are instructive in demonstrating the degree to which our every
word and action affects our social environment. The fact is, however, that
we're usually so busy thinking about being judged ourselves ("Do they like
me? Will I fit in? Should I laugh at that joke? Was it actually a joke?"), that
we don't take the opportunity to learn as much as we can about the peo-

ple around us. The same holds true in business situations. How often in business meetings do we step back from our own agenda to see what our business partners, clients, and colleagues' behavior and language are communicating about who they are? And how much more productive would we be if we did it more often?

Conclusion:
Unleashed!
The high calling of coaching

Stepping Up to the Challenge

There *is* a war for talent, and as the baby boomers continue to leave the corporate world, the need for qualified leaders who can attract and develop talent will only grow. It is a war that will be won by those unique and special individuals who can coach others to their highest performance and unleash their talent upon their organizations. As an organizational leader, you are on the front lines.

And as a leader in your organization, you will increasingly be called upon to play a different role in the lives of your colleagues—you will be asked to be a coach. Coaching is a high calling—every day I work with people who are dedicated to developing themselves and improving their leadership effectiveness and who let me be a part of that process. They give me access to their most guarded thoughts and feelings, and I have been privileged to watch them soar to previously unknown heights. When I set out to write *Unleashed!,* I wanted to share the secret of what I and other professional coaches do to foster exceptional performance in the clients with whom we work. What is this secret? The secret is that there isn't one! There is no technique or series of tried-and-true questions you can ask in order to coach others for significantly higher levels of sustained performance. Stepping into the role of coach will require you to change. It will require that you begin with yourself and be honest with your intentions for others.

Everything you needed to know about how to coach you already knew prior to reading this book. You knew it because you have either had the gift of a coach-like individual in your professional history, or at the very least, you have experienced its opposite and know first hand what is ineffective.

The challenge lies in actually doing what you know. As with so many other things in life, it is not a matter of gaining new knowledge, but rather, it is about being disciplined and putting into practice those things you already know in theory.

Coaching takes place through the interaction of three timeless principles: **Earning the Right to Coach, A Perfect Partnership,** and **Dangerous Conversations.** If you were looking for an easy, step-by-step process, then this book will have been disappointing. However, if you can recognize the fundamental truth behind these principles, and are willing to live them more intentionally, I believe you will reach a level of success you had not anticipated. Because when you forget to think about your own success, and no longer make everything about you, success will be yours. And ultimately, success will be the Talent's.

Perhaps the most surprising thing people learn when they begin to coach is that being a great Leader Coach is more about who *you* are as a person than any one thing you could ever actually do. Earning the Right to Coach requires you to focus on being the kind of person others want to invite into their lives. Once you accept that you have created every relationship you have, you will no longer be able to hide from your own contribution.

If you are authentic, hold yourself in high esteem, and enter the coaching relationship with noble intentions, you will be welcomed into the lives of others as someone they trust to assist their development. I call this dynamic, Talent-focused relationship A Perfect Partnership. You don't need to become an expert in the Talent's life. You do, however, need to see him for his very best, confront him with that version of himself, and hold him accountable for demonstrating this potential. Change is achieved in this partnership by engaging in Dangerous Conversations. As coaches, we are charged with making the Talent expand his perspective (challenge his thinking) and then his comfort zone (take new actions). You will do this by asking him provocative, challenging questions, and then holding his feet to the fire when he tries to turn away.

Organizations today are starved for talent and are desperately in need of leaders who can unlock the potential of their people. This is your job. What you need to unleash high performance within your organization is within you. It is time for you to step up. I wrote this book not for you, but for all the lives you have the privilege of touching. May you never take this for granted!

"How we spend our days, is of course, how we spend our lives."

Annie Dillard

AfterWords

The genesis of this work was Gregg and I setting out to develop a high impact, experiential coach training program for the wonderful clients we work with at Bluepoint Leadership Development. Over the course of two years of challenging personal explorations, countless discarded drafts, and numerous dangerous conversations, we developed the *Great Expectations Coaching Model*. We wrote *Unleashed!* to share with you what we learned, and we hope that you have been as blessed in reading it as we have been in writing it.

We have had the good fortune of meeting and speaking with hundreds of people who generously shared their coaching stories and have told us how they have applied the principles of the Great Expectations model. If you have a coaching story, or you simply want to share your thoughts after reading the book, we would love to hear from you. We also invite you to attend a *Leader as Coach Workshop*—for more information visit bluepointleadership.com

Please email us at greggthompson@bluepointleadership.com or susannebiro@bluepointleadership.com

Warmly,
Susanne Biro

Endnotes

1 Steve Crabtree, "Getting Personal in the Workplace," *Gallup Management Journal,* June 6, 2004.

2 R. Rosenthal and L. Jacobson, *Pygmalion in the Classroom,* (New York: Rinehart and Winston, 1968).

3 Robert Tauber, *Self-Fulfilling Prophecy: A Guide to Its Use in Education,* (Westport, CT: Greenwood Publications, 1997).

4 Marcus Buckingham, *Now, Discover Your Strengths,* (New York: The Free Press, 2001).

5 Thomas Szasz, *Heresies,* (New York: Doubleday, 1976).

6 Paul Pearsall, *Toxic Success: how to stop striving and start thriving,* (Inner Ocean Publishing: Makawao, HI: Inner Ocean Publishing, 2002).

7 Jon Kabat-Zinn, *Wherever You Go, There You Are,* (New York: Hyperion, 1994)

8 Henry Kissinger, *Years of Upheaval,* (Boston: Little Brown, 1982).

9 Rosabeth Moss Kanter. *Confidence: How Winning Streaks & Losing Streaks Begin & End.* (New York: Crown, 2004).

10 Jaya Chaliah and Edward Le Joly (eds), *A Guide to Daily Living with Mother Teresa—The Joy in Loving*, (Penguin: New York, 1997).

11 C. R. Rogers, *On Becoming a Person: A Therapist's View of Psychotherapy,* (London: Constable and Company Ltd., 1961).

12 ibid

13 David L. Cooperrider and Suresh Srivastva, "Appreciative Inquiry in Organizational Life," *Research in Organizational Change and Development,* (1987, Vol.1), pp 129-169.

14 ibid

15 ibid

16 Martin Gladwell, *Blink: The Power of Thinking without Thinking,* (New York: Little, Brown & Co., 2005).

17 Eric Berne, *Games People Play: The Basic Handbook of Transactional Analysis,* (New York: Ballantine Books, 1964).

18 Arbinger Institute, The. *Leadership and Self-Deception,* (San Francisco: Berrett-Koehler, 2000).

19 J. Luft, *Group processes: An introduction to group processes,* (Mountain View, CA: Mayfield, 1970).

Index